D0393614

# WILDFLOWERS

## OF THE SMOKIES

LEAD AUTHOR: PETER WHITE

CO-AUTHORS:
TOM CONDON, JANET ROCK, CAROL ANN McCORMICK,
PAT BEATY, KEITH LANGDON

GREAT SMOKY MOUNTAINS
ASSOCIATION
Gatlinburg, Tennessee

EDITED BY: Don DeFoe & Steve Kemp
DESIGNED BY: Christina Watkins
ILLUSTRATED BY: Nancy O'Hare & Joey Heath
PROJECT COORDINATION BY: Steve Kemp
TYPOGRAPHY BY: Coralie Bloom
INVALUABLE ASSISTANCE BY: Judy Collins, Lynne Davis,
Donna Groat, Jo Hoy & Glenn Taylor
COVER PHOTOGRAPH BY: Bill Lea
SECOND EDITION PRODUCTION BY: Lisa Horstman
PRINTED IN HONG KONG

7   8   9

ISBN 0-937207-20-9

GREAT SMOKY MOUNTAINS
ASSOCIATION

Great Smoky Mountains Association is a nonprofit organization
which supports the educational, scientific, and historical programs of
Great Smoky Mountains National Park. Our publications are an educational service intended to enhance the public's understanding and
enjoyment of the national park. If you would like to know more
about our publications, memberships, and projects, please contact:
Great Smoky Mountains Association, 115 Park Headquarters Road,
Gatlinburg, TN 37738  (865) 436-7318. www.SmokiesStore.org

We dedicate this book to the many people who love the wildflowers of Great Smoky Mountains National Park and support their conservation. More particularly, we dedicate this book to: Arthur Stupka who, as an employee of the National Park Service, made substantial contributions to our knowledge of the natural history of the Smokies and who made countless observations on the distribution, blooming, and ecology of the park's wildflowers, and to Professors Aaron J. Sharp and Edward E. C. Clebsch, whom we choose because of their own special contributions and because they represent the many teachers and researchers whose love of and knowledge of the wildflowers of the Smokies have inspired generations of students with the beauty, wonder, and scientific interest of Smokies wildflowers, thereby contributing to their conservation; and to our own representatives of the next generation of Smokies lovers, our children, Alanna Susan Beaty, Andrew Jason Beaty, Tyler James Beaty, Fraser Daniel Langdon, Torrey Mather Langdon, Rose Lorraine Peifer, Lily Claire McCormick, Matthew Trillium Hanlin White, and Sarah Linnaea Hickler White.

# CONTENTS

# INTRODUCTION

Great Smoky Mountains National Park is a world-renowned preserve of wildflower diversity. In our introduction to this flowering landscape, we will describe why the park is so diverse in flowers, tell you some of the exciting stories behind the wildflowers, outline the value of this diversity, and describe the challenges that park conservationists face in insuring that plants in the Great Smokies will be preserved unimpaired for the enjoyment of future generations.

# A WONDROUS DIVERSITY

The diversity of plants in the Smokies is dazzling——some 1,500 kinds of flowering plants are found in Great Smoky Mountains National Park, more than in any other North American national park, even though a number of other parks are considerably larger. Globally, this diversity also stands out. The southern Appalachians are one of the temperate zone's hot spots for plants. In fact, north of the tropics, only China has more species. Of course, the tropical rain forests are unsurpassed in the total number of species, but those forests are dominated by woody plants—trees, shrubs, and woody vines. Plants we might call "wildflowers" in the normal sense of the word, like bromeliads and orchids, occur in tropical rain forests mostly high in the forest canopy on tree branches. From this perspective, the wildflower diversity of the Smokies is unrivaled even there.

The wildflowers of the Smokies are also spectacular as individual species—we hope this book will help you become acquainted with such delights as the ten species of trillium, some 30 species of native orchids, the spring ephemerals like Dutchman's britches and spring-beauty, the fall asters and goldenrods, and many more.

Why are there so many species in the Smokies? Explanations involve climate, habitat diversity, geological history, climatic changes, and the conservation effort that resulted in the creation of the national park.

## CLIMATE & HABITAT DIVERSITY . . . . . . . . . . .

The climate of the park encompasses a range of conditions from warm to cool temperate, but rainfall is everywhere abundant. We know that plant diversity tends to increase from cooler to warmer parts of the world and from drier to wetter climates—so the Smokies sit midway on the temperature gradient and definitely at the wet end of the rainfall gradient. The lack of a dry season and the abundance of moisture and humidity, especially during the summer growing season, create conditions that are good for plant growth.

The vegetation pattern of the Smokies has been called the most complex in all of North America. Differences in elevation and the ruggedness of the mountains result in a wide variety of environments that produce a wide variety of vegetation. The two most important factors are elevation and topographic features that affect soil moisture.

Elevation ranges from about 850 feet in the southwest corner of the park to 6,643 feet on Clingmans Dome, the third highest peak in the East. As one moves from lower to higher elevations, the climate becomes cooler and wetter and cloud cover is more frequent. The frost-free season ranges from over 200 days at the lower elevations to some 100 days at the higher elevations. Rainfall ranges from about 55 inches at the low elevations to over 90 inches on the high peaks.

Slope aspect (the compass direction a slope faces), slope position (the distance between stream valley and ridge), and slope shape (the convexity or concavity of a slope) all combine to determine the amount of sunlight reaching a site, its warmth, and its ability to retain soil moisture. At mid- and lower elevations, soil moisture is critical. Rainfall is high, but rain runs off of ridges and convex landforms and flows into the concave mountain valleys that are referred to as "coves." The more convex slopes farther from valleys are drier and the concave slopes and valleys are moister.

South and west facing slopes get more sunlight during the warmer parts of the day and evaporation is higher. Ridges are exposed to sunlight more hours of the day; narrow valleys and north facing slopes can be shaded for much of the day. Variation in these factors becomes less important as you go to higher elevations—there the temperature is cooler, rainfall more abundant, and cloud cover more frequent, so topographic variation in soil moisture is less of a factor in plant distribution.

Many park trails pass repeatedly from stream valley or cove to open slope to ridge and back into the cove. Even if you stay within a narrow elevation range, the habitat changes dramatically. And because habitat changes, the species of trees and wildflowers you see vary also. This variety over short distances is one of the most distinctive features of plant diversity in the Smokies. When you put elevation and topography together, the diversity of habitats encompasses the diversity of forests found over much of the eastern United States.

Much of the park is underlaid by sandstones and other relatively acid bedrocks, but several important areas of limestone in the northwest part of the park add to habitat diversity. Limestone soils are rich in calcium and lower in acidity than other soils. Other habitat features that support unusual species are wetlands at the lower elevations, seepage areas (where spring water comes to the ground surface), open rock outcrops, boulder fields, and cliff faces.

## ICE AGES & LIFE ON THE ROCKS. . . . . . . . . . . .

Changing climates of the last ice age contributed to plant

diversity in a number of ways. Although the climate did become considerably cooler, these mountains, unlike the northern Appalachians, were not covered by the most recent advance of glacial ice (continental ice sheets reached as far south as the Ohio River Valley and northern Pennsylvania). Although climate change did cause some species to migrate over large distances, and there must have been some species extinction, the effects were not as drastic here as they were in those areas buried by ice.

Some species found today in the highest elevations have been in this area for tens of thousands of years. They did not have to migrate great distances to reach the Smokies and they could undergo evolution in this setting.

The changes that did occur during the ice age may have increased the number of endemics in the southern Appalachians (that is, species found nowhere else in the world). This happened in two ways. First, endemics arose simply because a species became restricted to one or a few populations, with all other populations of that species becoming extinct. In other words, some southern species could potentially cover a much wider range— for example, in the northern Appalachians if planted there—but they were restricted to small areas during the last ice age and never rebounded.

Second, endemics can evolve when small populations are genetically isolated from one another and the bulk of a species range. These populations have the chance to diverge, eventually producing several descendant species from one ancestral one. Whatever the cause, the southern Appalachians are not only known for their total diversity, but also for their highly restricted species—species that are restricted to the southern mountains, including some that are restricted to small areas within the mountains. The park has one plant, Rugel's ragwort, that occurs nowhere else in the world and a number of other species that are restricted to the park and its immediate surroundings.

The high elevation rock outcrops and cliffs of the Smokies

harbor species which tell a tale about past climate changes. In today's climates, the mountains are not high enough for a true alpine treeline—the tallest summits are covered with trees and the few open grassy areas that exist (called here "grassy balds") are not true alpine communities. However, during the height of the last ice age, the climate was cold enough for a treeline and alpine barrens above that line. At that time the general vegetation pattern was rather like that of Mt. Washington, New Hampshire, today. A remnant of the alpine flora can be found on high elevation and isolated cliff faces in the park like those on Mt. Le Conte. Here are some of the rarest species in the park, including a few species that occur above treeline in New England and range into the Canadian arctic.

## PROTECTION OF WILDFLOWERS, OLD-GROWTH FORESTS, & THE ECOLOGICAL WEB OF LIFE . . . . .

A final reason for the high diversity of Smokies wildflowers is conservation.

In the park archives is a faded pamphlet entitled "Save Our Mountains." This sounds like a modern rallying cry for preservation, but the pamphlet was published in 1926 during efforts to create a national park in the southern Appalachians. What were they trying to save the mountains from?

A full tilt logging boom between 1885 and 1939 trimmed the Great Smoky Mountains of much of their timber. Although it brought a significant influx of cash into the local economies, it also brought environmental havoc. Over 20 lumber companies and dozens of sawmills operated in what is now the national park. Clearcutting was the rule of the day and some companies cut from the river valleys all the way to the highest ridges.

However, the effort to create Great Smoky Mountains National Park was successful and the park was established in 1934. At that point, about a quarter of the park had not been significantly disturbed by farming or logging. The soils of such places harbor plants, animals, rich organic matter, and plant nutrients that had been removed from eroded areas.

The park has one of the largest tracts of old-growth forest left in the eastern United States and some of the best wildflower spots are in those old growth areas. More than large trees are protected when these remnants of primitive America are saved.

Even as you admire the Smokies' plant diversity and wild-flowers, it is important to recognize that conservation in the park protects not only the plant itself but the web of species inter-actions which is essential to this diversity. Plant diversity requires a diversity of pollinators, seed dispersers, and even fungi. For example, it is known that many plants must form a close association with soil fungi in order to extract nutrients from the soil.

Perhaps most dramatic is the case of orchids. Their minute seeds contain little in the way of nutrients for the orchid seedling. The seeds germinate deep in the soil and the seedlings live in close association with soil fungi before emerging as photo-synthetic orchids years later.

Wildflowers in the Smokies occur in natural populations that can harbor considerable genetic diversity. Sometimes this genetic variation shows up as variation in flower colors or leaf shape or plant size. Some trillium populations have a tremendous range of forms and colors. To see the effect of genetic differences in plant size, compare the most common woodland form of smooth Solomon's seal (one foot tall) with its relative the great Solomon's seal (three feet tall), which differs from it only in chromosome number. Just as species diversity is important to an ecosystem, genetic diversity within and among populations is important to a species.

Few people appreciate that Great Smoky Mountains National Park is more than just its list of wildflower species—it is the genetic diversity within wildflower populations and the complex interactions among plants, animals, fungi, and the envi-ronment.

# WILDFLOWER SEASONS

From the earliest hepaticas or spring-beauties in late winter to the last asters in late fall, there is a sequence of bloom among Smokies wildflowers. Blooming time, in addition to habitat, is another way that species specialize. The elevation range of the Smokies complicates seasonal classification, however. A given spring-blooming species will flower earliest at lower elevations because seasonal warming proceeds upwards from valleys to peaks.

Different patterns of blooming also characterize different habitats. For example, fall blooming members of the Aster family are prominent in dry forests—and those tend to have more shrubs and fewer herbaceous (non-woody) wildflowers in their understories than moister forests. But the most dramatic evolutionary lesson that wildflowers tell us has to do with the herbaceous wildflowers of moist, nutrient-rich sites, under deciduous trees.

## SPRING EPHEMERALS, DECIDUOUS TREES & ANTS

Ecologists speak of a group of species with similar broad adaptations as a "guild." In this sense, a special group of wildflowers called the spring ephemerals constitute a guild.

Ephemerals are so named because they appear above ground only in the early spring—they flower and fruit and then die back all in a two month period. They emerge in March or April, depending on the elevation, and they are gone by May or June. Some of these species give us the year's first "fall" color—in May (for example, the leaves of Dutchman's britches can turn a pastel yellow). By summer, the ephemerals have no leaves or other structures above ground—the warmest and wettest conditions are still ahead, but they are dormant and below ground!

This remarkable group of plants is adapted to the rhythm of

the overstory trees, a rhythm which also has implications for soil moisture and nutrients. And then there is a connection to ants as well.

The ephemerals appear before the leafing out of the deciduous trees, when full sunlight is streaming to the forest floor. This is also a time when soil moisture is high (because it is still cool and trees are not yet transpiring the great amount of water into the atmosphere that will give the Smokies their distinctive haze) and soil nutrients are plentiful (because of the decomposition of the tree leaves that fell the previous fall). Light, moisture, and nutrients are at high levels. The ephemerals exploit these conditions——they flower, fruit, and their above-ground parts decay. As the overstory leafs out, they are experiencing their autumn.

When considering spring ephemerals, however, a number of questions arise.

First, if an ephemeral can green out along the forest floor, why can't trees also unfurl their leaves? The answer probably lies in the way air temperature fluctuates—because the moist earth buffers the extremes of day and night temperatures, plants can leaf out near the ground sooner than they can at three feet or ten feet or 150 feet above the ground. At greater heights, the days may actually be warmer than at ground level, but the nights are colder and still experience killing frosts. Supporting this reasoning is the observation that the earliest spring-leafing plants are close to the ground and wildflowers get taller as the spring season progresses. Even within one group of spring plants, earlier species are shorter and later species taller. Compare the early yellow violet with its fleshy leaves pressed to the ground to the upright Canadian violet that comes later.

So, we may have explained why spring ephemerals put out their leaves so early, but why do they also bloom in the early part of the year?

The reasons here are probably twofold. If a plant leafs and flowers in different seasons then it has the problem of storing energy until flowering time, but if it does both at once, its leaves transfer energy-rich compounds directly to reproduction. There probably is a cost and a risk to storage, but it is important to note that some species have indeed separated flowering from leafing. Ramps put out green leaves in spring; these die back and the plant flowers in the summer with no leaves at all. There are two wild orchids that do the same thing—crane-fly orchid and Adam-and-Eve orchid—but these species go one step further. They put out leaves in the fall and lose them in the spring (they then flower in summer without leaves). They are truly backwards plants—backwards to the seasons by leafing from November to May, rather than the other way around.

Fringed phacelia tells a similar backwards story—but here the plant germinates in the fall (in a landscape dominated by trees that can reach 400 years of age, this species, amazingly, is a winter annual), forms a green carpet for winter, and then a white carpet of flowers in spring—before it goes entirely to seed.

There is another reason to fruit in spring. Many ephemeral seeds are ant dispersed. They have special adaptations to attract ants who carry their seeds to new places, even planting them in or on the mineral soil. Often the seeds carry a special oil body that is especially attractive to ants. Spring seems to be a good time to be ant dispersed.

The best places to find good spring wildflower displays are moist slope positions—lower slopes and coves—in deciduous forests and particularly in the park's old-growth watersheds. You will see the forest floor covered like a blanket with a diversity of flowers—and you will see the early spring insects out busily visiting them.

# WILDFLOWER ISLANDS

The Smoky Mountains contain several isolated habitats that are home to surprising species.

Capping the upper elevations of the Smoky Mountains are

evergreen forests of spruce and fir. These forests, now under severe threat in the Smokies because of a non-native insect and air pollution, range along the Appalachians from North Carolina and Tennessee to eastern Canada. They are related to similar forests of spruce and fir that stretch across Canada in a great arc known as the Boreal (northern) Forest. Wildflowers of these forests in the Smokies include northern plants far south of their main range—plants like bluebead lily and wood sorrel.

Moving up in elevation is like moving north in latitude (in both directions it gets cooler)—but it is not identical. Smoky Mountain spruce-fir forests are not simply an outlier of northern forests. For example, the growing season is longer farther south and the winters are not as cold. Spruce-fir forests have their own distinctive features, including Catawba rhododendron in the understory, with its purple flowers, and endemic species not found in the north, like Rugel's ragwort and skunk goldenrod.

If the spruce-fir forests tell a northern story, the cliff faces at high elevations tell an arctic story. As described earlier, a few species in these habitats are found in the arctic or above treeline in the New England mountains. With them are distinctive southern Appalachian endemics like the mountain avens.

The limestone districts—Cades Cove, Whiteoak Sink, Rich Mountain Gap, and several smaller areas—harbor a flora that is distinctive because of the bedrock. Because limestone becomes more frequent towards the Midwest, some of these species are at the eastern limits of their range. Such species include climbing bittersweet, blazing star, Virginia bluebell, and yellow mandarin.

A final geographical story has its origins in deeper evolutionary and geological history. A number of our Smokies wildflowers have their closest relatives not in the Rocky Mountains or other parts of North America, not in Europe, but half a world away in eastern Asia. Examples are many, but consider the barberry family: may-apple, blue cohosh, and umbrella leaf are species of plants that are found only in two isolated areas: eastern North America and eastern Asia. Among the trees, the magnolias and tuliptree show the same pattern.

The explanation here is continental drift, changing climates, and descent from common ancestors. These plants are representatives of a flora that was once found in the far north (when the climate was warmer millions of years ago) and occurred across landbridges that joined North America, Northern Europe, and Siberia. Populations had genetic contact across this area as recently as about 10 million years ago. The continents eventually drifted apart and climates cooled. In both North America and Eurasia, continental interiors became dry and the remnants of the once widespread flora moved eastward to rest against the eastern coastlines of the two North Temperate continents. Here moisture is more dependable because storms come from the west, south, and even the east. Some species did persist in northern Europe (hepatica is an example) and/or the Pacific Northwest (trillium is an example), but the southern Appalachians and mountains at comparable latitudes in east Asia became the world's centers of diversity of North Temperate plants.

## RARE PARK WILDFLOWERS · · · · · · · · · · · · · · ·

Great Smoky Mountains National Park has over 300 rare plant species. Surprisingly, this number represents almost one quarter of the park's native flora. The term rare can have many meanings, but species that are rare are usually those that have small populations and small geographic ranges.

Of the Smokies' rare plants, as many as 125 appear on the protected plant lists of either North Carolina or Tennessee. They are given special protection by these states because of their rarity or because they suffer from particular threats such as habitat loss or non-native insect attack. Some plants, including ginseng and pink lady's slipper, are given special attention because of their commercial value. They are subject to exploitation even within Great Smoky Mountains National Park.

Some of the Smokies' rare plants are federally listed under

the Endangered Species Act. These are critically threatened plants which may become extinct or disappear from much of their range if not immediately protected. Currently the park has three plant species afforded this highest protection; they are mountain avens, an Endangered high elevation herb; Virginia spiraea, a Threatened flowering shrub of rocky streamsides; and the Endangered rock gnome lichen.

The park has 12 additional species of special concern—that is, species under review for federal listing. Special concern species require more information on biological status and threats, but listing at the federal level is probably appropriate based on current information.

## SPECIES OF SPECIAL CONCERN

**Fraser fir (*Abies fraseri*)**
*Habitat*: Above 5,000 feet.
*Notes*: Great Smokies comprise almost 75% of the entire range of this southern Appalachian endemic.
**Cain's reed bent grass (*Calamagrostis cainii*)**
*Habitat*: Cliffs and landslide scars, high elevation.
*Notes*: Great Smokies comprise most of the range of this southern Appalachian endemic.
**Mountain bittercress (*Cardamine clematitis*)**
*Habitat*: Cool mossy springs and seeps, mid to high elevations.
*Notes*: A southern Appalachian endemic.
**Glade spurge (*Euphorbia purpurea*)**
*Habitat*: Moist woods, igneous rock at mid elevation.
*Notes*: Rare throughout its limited range.
**Smoky Mountain manna grass (*Glyceria nubigena*)**
*Habitat*: Trailside seeps, balds, and roadsides above 5,000 feet.
*Notes*: A southern Appalachian endemic, only one location known from outside Smokies.
**Carolina one-flowered rush (*Juncus trifidus ssp. carolinianus*)** *Habitat*: Cliff ledges, high elevation.

*Notes:* Disjunct from the north. Possibly extirpated from the Smokies.

**Butternut (*Juglans cinerea*)**
*Habitat:* Rocky streamsides, rich soil. Low to mid elevations.
*Notes:* A wide-spread northeastern tree becoming rare over much of its range due to a non-native canker-causing fungus.

**Gray's lily (*Lilium gray*)**
*Habitat:* Open woods and balds; mid to high elevation. This southern Appalachian endemic. was collected in the Smokies in 1891. The exact location of the collection is not known. Possibly extirpated.

**Fraser's loosetrife (*Lysimachia fraseri*)**
*Habitat:* Roadsides and openings on steep wooded slopes.
*Notes:* This southern Appalachian endemic was collected "near Gatlinburg" in 1935. Possibly extirpated.

**Rugel's ragwort (*Rugelia nudicaulis*)**
*Habitat:* Rich moist woods, usually in spruce-fir forests.
*Notes:* A Smokies endemic.

**Rock skullcap (*Scutellaria saxatilis*)**
*Habitat:* Slopes and trailsides; low elevation.
*Notes:* At the southern limit of its range.

**Mountain catchfly (*Silene ovata*)**
*Habitat:* Moist coves, oakwoods, light gaps; mid elevation.
*Notes:* A southeastern species, threatened by habitat loss throughout its range.

Almost all of the Smokies' rare plants can be placed into one of three plant distribution categories: endemic species (species restricted to a small area), disjunct species (outlying populations of species separated by a great distance from their main range), and peripheral species (species at the edge of their range).

About 30 percent of the park's rare plants are southern Appalachian endemics (found only here). These plants are usually found in special habitats, such as rocky outcrops on the highest peaks or high elevation grassy balds and landslide scars.

Endemics have fewer populations than species with large ranges, placing them at long-term risk of extinction, not to mention the genetic loss that occurs when individual populations are lost.

Some of the park's most fascinating southern Appalachian endemics are found high up. Mountain avens is one. In the Smokies it grows on vertical ledges above 6,000 feet where it receives very little competition from other plant species and considerable moisture from dense fog. Its habitat is so specialized that only eleven populations of mountain avens are known to exist in the world. Even more amazing, Great Smoky Mountains National Park has one plant species that has not been found beyond park boundaries: Rugel's ragwort, a member of the Aster family, found mostly above 4,000 feet. Another grass with a very narrow range, Cain's reed bent grass, was believed to exist only on Mt. Le Conte until the discovery of a small population near Mt. Mitchell in 1991. Smoky Mountain manna grass is also confined to the park and one small area outside.

Peripherals comprise 40 percent of the park's rare plants. Many of these are northern species at the southern limit of their range and are found on the highest mountain peaks in the park. Since these plants are at the southern edge of their range, they are exposed to a different set of environmental conditions than are found elsewhere. These include differences in rainfall, temperature, even air pollution and global warming. These factors can limit range expansion and in some cases increase mortality and decrease reproduction. Peripheral species may be at great risk from changes in the environment. An example of a peripheral species is rose twisted-stalk. This plant is at the southern limit of its range in the Smokies where it can only survive in cool, high elevation forests.

Plants that are disjunct from their main range make up about 20 percent of the park's rarest species and are at risk because of their genetic isolation. Some disjuncts are relicts from earlier times when the climate was much cooler and glaciers blanketed the northern portions of the continent. Linear-leaved gentian is an excellent example. This rare northern wildflower occurs on Mt. Le Conte, but that is the only known location of the plant south of Pennsylvania.

# THE VALUE OF DIVERSITY

Ecologists call the number of species in an area species "richness" and as we have seen, the park is rich indeed. This is a good choice of terms—for species diversity means richness in quite another sense as well.

The national park is a protected reserve of the genetic and species diversity of plants, animals, and other organisms. Why is this diversity important? Some argue that the species we share the planet with should be respected—that they have rights of existence, too. In addition to those kinds of arguments, biological diversity directly supports human quality and quantity of life. Not surprisingly, the National Cancer Institute and other groups have repeatedly visited the Smokies to take, under permit, small plant samples, looking for new medicines, for better forest trees, for ornamental plants for our gardens, and for other uses.

To illustrate this point, consider the may-apple. This attractive but unassuming wildflower was used by Native Americans to treat warts; now it is used as the source of medicine to fight various cancers. Fully, 25 percent of our prescription drugs still contain at least one ingredient taken directly from a higher plant.

Often traditional cultures had a relatively well-defined knowledge of the plants and animals around them. The Cherokee are no exception—over 600 species from these mountains were, or still are, used as medicines by the Cherokee. An equal number of species was used for a huge array of other purposes—dyes, body paint, poisons for hunting and fishing, building materials, foods, chewing gum, and materials for rope and baskets. The Cherokee had documented uses for 60 percent of the flora of this diverse region. This represents a tremendous botanical knowledge. No, not all Cherokee uses would find parallels today—and not all their medicines worked. But through generations of trial and error their uses represent a refined knowledge of plant biochemistry and the potential for use. A recent study showed that the study of traditional cultural use of plants was a faster route to discovering new medicines than blind screening of all plants in an area.

The discovery of a new medicine from a plant today does not represent its final "value" to people—the new diseases of the future, the new challenges of the future, are unknown. But diversity itself represents a hedge against future uncertainty. When you add to the permanent potential that biological diversity represents, the pleasure of plant beauty, and the enjoyment of plants within this remnant of wilderness America, the value of a rich landscape like Great Smoky Mountains National Park is immeasurable.

# CONSERVING WILDFLOWERS

Conservation in the Smokies began with the creation of the national park in 1934, but the story doesn't end there. In the early 1800s, human-caused disturbances were relatively mild—only the best specimens of the more valuable trees like black cherry, black walnut, and white ash were harvested. Soon, however, the productive lower coves were entirely deforested and cultivated for crops.

By the turn of the century, corporate logging came to the Smokies, using railroads and thousands of workers. Hundreds of square miles, including most of the remaining cove hardwoods, were mass harvested in a short period of time. Old photographs show stumps, some brush, and not much else across whole watersheds. The moist and cool forest floor became sunny, hot, and dry—and the profusion of shade-loving wildflowers disappeared. On some slopes logging slash fires were followed by soil erosion.

Today, some of the most drastically affected sites in the park are still without a complete tree cover after seventy years. And despite decades of protection and recovery, it is still rare to find such species as dwarf ginseng, Fraser's sedge, or large populations of white trillium in the second-growth forests of the park. These species take many years to flower, produce few flowers and seeds each year, and, thus, have limited abilities to reclaim these damaged areas.

In the sites that were saved from logging and farming, the soils were never exposed to drying and erosion and were never turned under by plows. The nutrients required for plant growth are released slowly by the decay of logs never removed by loggers. The diverse ground flora blooms as it has for thousands of years. For the damaged sites, only future generations will get to see the wildflower displays that once occurred.

The "prime directive" of all national parks is to preserve not only native species, but the natural processes that maintain them. We used to think that meant protecting parks from all disturbances, but we realize now that some disturbances are natural. Among the first steps in conserving national parks and similar reserves should be to study natural areas to understand what is, indeed, natural.

# DEATH BY LACK OF FIRE . . . . . . . . . . . . . . .

While the park slowly recovers from the mass logging of the early 20th century, another threat to park resources, ironically, springs from efforts to protect the forests. Following large-scale logging, wildfires were common. These fires spread more rapidly, burned much hotter, and covered more ground than pre-logging era wildfires.

Public concern led to the formation of wildfire control organizations, especially on lands administered by government agencies. Government policy nationwide began treating the wildfire issue as "...the moral equivalent of war." All fires were suppressed, even lightning-caused fires in communities of plants and animals that had been experiencing natural fires for thousands of years. In these habitats, the plants and animals have not only evolved to tolerate certain types of fire, many cannot thrive without it. Originally, natural fires occurred as a result of lightning strikes (the park averages about two such fires per year) as well as from fires set by Native Americans. Pollen and charcoal analysis of sediments in a pond in Cades Cove indicates a dramatic increase in fires about 2,000 years ago, during Indian times.

The Smokies' dry forests are found most commonly in the west end of the park, including several types of pine and/or oak forests on upper slopes and ridges that depend on occasional fire. In most cases, natural fires were different in quality and quantity from logging slash fires. Natural fires burned less intensely but more frequently, leaving fewer branches, dead needles, and forest litter as fuel for the next fire. Most of the plant species in these dry forests easily survive low-intensity fires where flames typically burn only a few inches high and usually consume only the top layer of forest floor litter.

With forest fuels kept to a low level, catastrophic fires are easily prevented. Natural fire also creates a more open, sunnier forest with regular pulses of fertilizer—nutrients released in the ash of dead branches and leaves.

Scores of wildflowers call the park's dry pine and oak forests home: many legumes such as goat's rue and partridge-pea, numerous members of the Aster family including purple creeping and stiff asters, grasses like Indiangrass and Elliott's bluestem, showy species—fringed polygala, Carolina lily, trailing arbutus, and orchids including the whorled pogonia and yellow-fringed orchid. These and other disturbance-dependent species are becoming restricted to trail edges or places where the occasional wildfire still occurs.

Fire management policies are changing and will eventually allow use of fires in a controlled manner. But these policies will not and should not be reversed wholesale overnight. High accumulations of fuel in some habitats will require careful removal by burning in the right season and under the right weather. And this time, as the policies change, a scientific monitoring system will guide park managers in their pursuit of ecological balance.

# WILD HOGS NOT WELCOME HERE . . . . . . . . . .

In the late 1940s, European wild hogs that had escaped from a game farm in North Carolina entered the park for the first time. Sporadic attempts to remove them failed and they soon spread throughout the Smokies. These large, non-native mammals became immediately unpopular by rooting up wildflowers and creating large "wallows" in virtually every lower elevation wetland.

Wild hogs routinely concentrate their rooting activities in beech gaps where spring beauties, trout lilies, and other spring wildflowers are abundant. They damage these unique forest types by rooting for bulbs and tubers as well as invertebrates, leaving the gaps looking like they've been freshly plowed. Beech gaps are dominated by American beech trees and occur up to 5,800 feet in elevation—making these stands the highest deciduous forests east of the Rockies. With an open understory and less acid soils than the surrounding spruce-fir stands, the beech areas offer a different flora that adds to the diversity of high elevation forests.

Grassy balds in the park, at least two of which (Gregory and Parson) probably predate European-American settlement, also receive periodic disturbance from hogs. The grassy balds' flora is injured, but seems vigorous enough in this moist, sunny environment to recover, and no plants on the balds or elsewhere in the park are confirmed to have been lost due to hog activity. Still, park officials are concerned about long-term effects of hogs on the native plants and animals of the park. Also worrisome is the potential of the wild boar to transport non-native plant seeds—especially those of Japanese grass—from wetland to wetland, and their known capacity as hosts to diseases that are excreted in their feces and are dangerous to humans.

Since the late 1980s, large numbers of hogs have been trapped or shot by park crews, but totally eliminating hogs from the park is currently impossible. Continued control efforts are necessary, however, to keep hog populations at a level that their damage to native park resources is minimized.

Coyotes are known to prey on wild hog piglets and red wolves are capable of taking a full-grown boar. By restoring a natural process (predation), we may have begun recovery of grassy balds, beech gaps, and wetlands.

## ALIENS IN THE FOREST . . . . . . . . . . . . . . . . .

When humans transport species across major barriers, like the oceans that separate the continents, they often court catastrophe. The Smokies have certainly had their share—the most important of these alien pests to date have affected forest trees, but changes to the forest canopy can also threaten wildflower populations along the forest floor.

The American chestnut was the largest of the dozen or so chestnut species in the world and it reached its greatest size within the southern mountains. By the 1920s, however, the Chinese chestnut blight, a species accidentally introduced into North America on imported Chinese chestnut trees, had reached the southern Appalachians. Complete mortality of large chestnut trees followed.

A similar story, and one with perhaps greater consequences for park wildflowers, is the invasion of the park by the balsam woolly adelgid, a tiny Eurasian insect. Although all true firs in North America can be attacked by the adelgid, Fraser fir, a narrow southern mountain endemic, is the most susceptible. Fraser fir dominated high mountain forests in the park with another evergreen, red spruce. When the park was created in 1934, conservationists had protected the largest block of old-growth spruce-fir forest then remaining in the eastern United States. Unfortunately, these forests were to be greatly altered by the arrival of the adelgid in the 1950s. The death of Fraser fir has been conspicuous in the park for the last several decades.

Undisturbed spruce-fir forests have dark, cool, and moist understories. There are only two dominant trees—and the large scale death of the fir allows light and wind to penetrate. Red spruce becomes vulnerable to wind throw, the soil surface dries, and shrubs become dense because of the added sunlight. These changes may cause a decline in the distinctive wildflowers of these high elevation forests, as well as other plants such as ferns, mosses and liverworts. At least eight nationally rare mosses and liverworts depend on Fraser fir bark, and one lichen and one spider species were recently listed as federally Endangered because of their dependence on this fast-changing habitat.

Dogwood anthracnose, a fungal disease of dogwoods, is believed to be from Asia. First found on both coasts of the U.S. in the late 1970s, the disease spread southward, reaching western North Carolina in 1987. Flowering dogwoods in cool, moist habitats are extremely susceptible, with whole stands dying within a few years. Massive losses occurred in the late 1980s and early 1990s, with at least one-third of the park's total population succumbing. Loss of the dogwood may influence light and microclimate in these forests. Because dogwood concentrate calcium in their leaves, they are important soil builders. No one knows what changes the loss of dogwood may bring to forest soils and wildflowers in the park.

As if these aliens weren't enough, there are others. Beech bark disease, caused by a scale insect and a fungus from Europe, was discovered in the park in 1993. Butternut canker, a fungus from Asia, is a chronic stem and twig disease of butternuts in the park. The east Asian hemlock woolly adelgid has become established in the middle Atlantic states and is making its way southward. The alien gypsy moth has been detected in the park, but has not yet caused widespread defoliation.

The succession of alien insects and diseases is being studied. The most promising lines of attack are biological control agents—reacquainting the pests with their own parasites and predators from overseas. Another focus of research is to develop resistance genetically within native plants. Alien species invasions are sometimes called biological pollution. Conservationists will have to deal with the changes these species cause in order to protect the original diversity of the park.

Plants from other continents are also a conservation issue in Great Smoky Mountains National Park. Most people are familiar with kudzu, but you probably won't spot it in the park. The park has over 100 known sites where kudzu has climbed over any living thing that couldn't move fast enough, but park crews have spent years controlling it with substantial success. Only a few stubborn sites remain.

Other pest species may be less familiar: oriental bittersweet, Japanese grass, princess tree, garlic mustard, and privet number among the 25 non-native pest plants of the park. These foreigners out-compete native plants in some sites, are persistent for decades once established, and are invasive of natural sites following natural disturbances. Non-native pest plants in particular are competitors of rare native plants that exist only in specialized habitats such as cliffs, floodplains, rock outcrops, and sunny glades. Another concern is that some are so closely related to native wildflowers that hybridization is a possibility.

# THE AIR THAT WILDFLOWERS BREATHE . . . . . .

It may come as a surprise, but even remote wilderness areas like the park can be impacted by air pollution. In fact, air masses from the southwest, west, and northwest bring air pollution exported from sites of production by tall smokestacks, as well as the pollution produced by the East's many automobiles. The high rainfall of the park is one of the ways that pollutants are deposited here.

The plants on the high peaks of the Smokies intercept more than their share of pollutants in the atmosphere. The two areas of greatest concern to wildflower enthusiasts are acid precipitation and ground level ozone pollution.

Acid precipitation originates from many sources, mostly "point sources" such as the smokestacks of power plants (often hundreds of miles away). Some of the highest rates of aerial deposition of nitrate in eastern North America occur on the peaks of Great Smoky Mountains National Park. The rain and especially fog at high elevations is very acidic. The direct effect of bathing plants in acid mists for many days of the year is compounded by the possible acidification of high elevation soils. The unbuffered acid may leach aluminum in soil water which in turn is taken up in plants, replacing calcium in cell walls. Eventually there may be less vigorous plants at the highest elevations— depending on geology. Ground level ozone pollution forms when certain gaseous emissions—mostly from automobiles—react with oxygen in sunlight. It is a highly reactive gas that at commonly reached levels will injure plant foliage—and human lungs. Ground level ozone should not be confused with damage to the earth's ozone layer, a different problem which affects the amount and type of sunlight which reaches the earth's surface.

Much experimental research has been conducted in the park on the ground level ozone pollution problem. As many as 30 native plant species are affected, including those wildflowers listed here. Still, less than seven percent of the park's native vascular plants have been tested for ozone injury.

# PLANT POACHERS. . . . . . . . . . . . . . . . .

Because Great Smoky Mountains National Park is America's most-visited national park, patrolling its vast area while looking after hoards of visitors is no small task for park rangers. Plant theft occurs here, and it occurs more frequently than anyone would prefer to tolerate.

| OZONE SENSITIVE PLANTS IN THE GREAT SMOKIES | | |
|---|---|---|
| COMMON NAME | SCIENTIFIC NAME | SENSITIVITY |
| Rugel's ragwort | *Rugelia nudiculis* | Moderate |
| White snakeroot | *Ageratina altissima* | Slight |
| Tall milkweed | *Asclepias exaltata* | Extreme |
| Black-eyed susan | *Rudbeckia hirta* | Extreme |
| Coneflower | *Rudbeckia laciniata* | Extreme |
| Opposite-leaved crown beard | *Verbesina occidentalis* | Extreme |
| Whorled wood aster | *Aster acuminatus* | Moderate |
| Mountain krigia | *Krigia montana* | Slight |
| Purple-stemmed aster | *Aster puniceus* | Slight |
| New York ironweed | *Vernonia noveboracensis* | Moderate |
| Indian Hemp | *Apocynum cannibivum* | Extreme |
| White wood aster | *Aster divaricatus* | Slight |

Gardeners dig up trilliums or columbines or yellow lady's slippers, mostly along park trails. Their acts have a direct negative effect on the park's flora and deprive others of enjoyment of their national park. Commercial poachers, though smaller in number, remove hundreds of plants per trip and probably make multiple trips in a year. Orchids, saleable perennials, conifer seedlings, and even log mosses have been poached for commercial purposes in the park, but by far the most illegal activity centers on a beautiful wildflower called American ginseng.

Collected for over two centuries now, this formerly abundant herb lives in excess of 40 years. Ginseng roots collected in late summer and fall are dried and sold to local dealers who in turn sell to exporters. Most of the roots are eventually exported to the People's Republic of China, where it is valued as a folk medicine and tonic. Local appalachian dealers pay diggers about $500 per pound of dried roots and the price increases each year. Ginseng, like mayapple, umbrella leaf, and the magnolias, is found only in east Asia and eastern North America. After centuries of collecting, the Chinese species of ginseng is already extremely rare in the wild. Legal harvest areas in North America (such as national forests) are becoming depleted and the national park is the largest "protected" reserve for American ginseng anywhere. Unfortunately, even here it is still uncommon to rare.

Because plant poaching is such a serious problem in the park (some teams of poachers have been apprehended with over 2,000 ginseng roots), all visitors are encouraged to report suspicious activities to the nearest ranger station.

What to do if you suspect poaching activity:

-Note time, place.

-Description of suspect(s), clothing, hats, type of boot tread.

-Description of packs, digging implements.

-Contact any local ranger station (see park folder).

-Call Park Headquarters communications office at (865) 436-1230 (some people now call from the backcountry using cellular phones!).

## CONSERVATION THROUGH PROPAGATION . . . . .

The economic law of supply and demand is playing a role in the conservation of native plants. Increased rarity often means higher prices and more people willing to risk poaching. Careful propagation of species usually means lower prices and therefore less collection from wild populations. And many native plant nurseries are doing just that.

Increasing numbers of gardeners want to grow native plants,

and this is a welcome trend, but how do you know where to get them? Don't assume that native plants offered for sale aren't wild-collected or even illegally taken. Always check the reputation of the company, and don't be fooled by "nursery grown" labels—this indicates only that the plants were grown for at least 12 months in a nursery. Look for "100% nursery propagated" or similar labels—and ask questions. Some species such as lady's slipper orchids and trilliums are extremely difficult to propagate, so if they are offered for sale, it should raise your suspicions. For a list of nurseries that propagate wildflowers, contact North Carolina Botanical Garden, CB# 3375, University of North Carolina, Chapel Hill, NC 27599-3375 (phone 919-962-0522).

Want to be a native plant conservation activist? Join your state native plant society, or the Eastern Native Plant Alliance.

Tennessee Native Plant Society
1172 S. Dry Valley Road
Cookeville, TN 38506

North Carolina Wildflower Preservation Society
c/o North Carolina Botanical Garden
CB #3375
University of North Carolina at Chapel Hill
Chapel Hill, NC 27599

Eastern Native Plant Alliance
Network News
P.O. Box 147
Hillsboro, MD 21641

# WILDFLOWER WATCHING IN THE SMOKIES

Wildflower watching in the Great Smoky Mountains National Park offers unsurpassed opportunities for enjoying the mountains. It can get you away from the crowds of visitors along the roads and into areas of incredible beauty. But it can also get you into trouble. For this reason, we offer some warnings to keep in mind while you seek out the flowers of the park.

**WEATHER**—The Great Smoky Mountains are the most massive range of mountains in the eastern United States. These gently rolling ridges look, from a distance, like a harmless and comfortable place. And, for the most part, they are. Yet, they can also be dangerous and unpredictable.

Wildflowers start blooming as early as February in the lower elevations. Winter has still not loosened its grip on the mountain peaks at this time. It may also make forays to the lower elevations. Sudden snowstorms have arisen as late as May. Spring wildflower enthusiasts should always be prepared for a sudden turn to cold, wet weather. Warm clothing and rain gear should be available at any time.

Spring flooding is also common during the peak wildflower season. Care should always be taken when fording rain swollen creeks. Plan your hikes to avoid such crossings, especially during heavy rains.

Summer hikers should be prepared for rain as well. At the higher elevations, up to 90 inches of precipitation fall every year. The lower elevations receive 50 inches yearly. The dense forests and numerous ridges of the Smokies can allow storms to sneak up and strike with very little warning. Be prepared at all times.

During thunderstorms, return to the safety of your automobile, if possible, or seek shelter in the deeper forest. Lightning is more likely to strike higher elevations, rocky outcrops, isolated trees in open areas, and along the edges between fields and forests.

The weather of autumn is perhaps the most predictable. Warm days and cool nights are the order of the day. Rain is less frequent, but still a possibility. An unprepared hiker caught in a fall rain shower could become a victim of hypothermia. This lowering of the body's core temperature can be life-threatening. Again, go prepared.

Winter temperatures and snow can come as early as Halloween, when the last of the asters are still in bloom. Conditions can be severe, especially at higher elevations.

**TRAILS**—Many park trails pass through very rugged country. The hiker needs to be aware of loose rocks, unbridged streams, and steep hillsides; all common features of mountain trails. Hikers should also carry a map and follow trail signs. Lost hikers have usually strayed from the maintained trails. Please stay on the trails and plan to be in camp or back to your car by dark. If children are accompanying you, equip them with a loud whistle and instruct them to sit and blow the whistle should they become separated from you.

**POISONOUS PLANTS**—Perhaps the most dreaded plant in the Smokies is poison ivy. It grows as a ground plant as well as a tree-hugging vine. The vine can be recognized by short black roots all along its length. These rootlets clasp the tree's bark for support and give the vine a hairy appearance. Although it has a very different appearance from the ground form, it is the same plant. Both forms have compound leaves with three palmately arranged leaflets. Perhaps you were taught "leaflets three, let it be" as a means of identification.

A rash is a result of an allergic reaction to the oils present in all parts of the plant. Some people are born very sensitive to these oils, while others will go through a longer period before they become sensitive. The more exposure you have to the oils, the more likely you will ultimately become sensitive. Since these oils are in the plant year-round, the plant should always be avoided. Should you come in contact with poison ivy, wash quickly with soap and water or swab the area with alcohol. Long pants and long-sleeved shirts will help you avoid getting oils on your skin, but remember to wash your clothing. Many a camper catches poison ivy from the oils on their clothing.

**SNAKES**—Whenever you go hiking in the Smokies you should keep one eye open for snakes. Most snakes will sense you coming and move off or simply hide, but occasionally, you will come across one. Of the 23 species of snakes found in the Smokies, only two are poisonous, the timber rattlesnake and the copper-head. These can be differentiated from the other non-poisonous snakes by examining the snake's head - from a distance. Both rattlesnakes and copperheads have triangular heads with an obvious "neck" between head and body. These snakes also have vertically slit pupils and heat sensing pits between their eyes and nostrils.

The timber rattlesnake is most often seen on dry rocky slopes or on the grassy balds. As their name implies, they rattle the horny plates at the end of their tail when disturbed. Unfortunately, they may not become disturbed until actually touched. Copperheads also tend to rattle their tails when disturbed. If they are in a pile of dry leaves, this will make them sound like a rattlesnake.

Both snakes rarely bite people unless provoked. To be sure that you do not disturb these animals, always watch where you put your feet and hands. Be careful also to look around before sitting on a rock, log, or the ground. If you should be bitten, cutting, sucking, and tourniquets are likely to do more harm than good. Calmly get out of the woods and to a ranger station or hospital. Also, it is not necessary to kill the snake. Neither the ranger nor the doctor needs to see it. Remember too, there has never been a documented case of a snake bite causing a human fatality in the Smokies.

**DANGEROUS INSECTS**—Without a doubt, bees, hornets, and wasps are the most dangerous animals in the Smokies. Every year, stings from these insects kill more people in the United States than snakes and bears combined. You can avoid bees by watching carefully for their hives and by taking a few simple precautions. Bees are attracted to the bright colors and sweet scents of many flowers. Wearing colorful clothing and perfumes can attract bees to you.

Yellowjackets are most active on dry slopes in the summer and early fall. Their nests are often found in the soft soils beside trails. Watch carefully for any activity along the trail. In the fall, bears seek out these nests for the protein-rich grubs. If you come across a recent bear attack on a yellowjacket nest, be very careful. The agitated wasps will swarm any disturbance.

People who are allergic to bee stings should carry a bee sting kit and teach those people with you how to use it. In severe cases, stings can cause anaphylactic shock, which can result in death. Immediate treatment with epinephrine is essential in these cases. For people who do not know if they are allergic, it is recommended that they carry over-the-counter antihistamines. These drugs are effective in reducing swelling, itchiness, and respiratory difficulties. If they should not relieve these conditions, medical treatment should be sought as quickly as possible.

**BEARS**—Estimates of bear populations in the Smokies place their numbers somewhere around 2,000 animals. Most visitors, however, will never see a bear. They are secretive animals which prefer to avoid human contact if possible. On the rare event that you should come across a bear while flower watching, follow these guidelines. First, be sure the bear knows where you are. Bears are more likely to be aggressive if startled. Observe bears from a distance, especially if cubs are present. If they know of your presence, they will either go about their business or move off. If you should come upon a bear that has become habituated to humans, it may act aggressively. This is likely to be around campgrounds and picnic areas. Because some thoughtless person has fed it, it may approach you for a handout. Do not continue the cycle of habituation by rewarding this bold behavior, it could ultimately lead to human injury or the death of the bear. Instead, shout at the bear, wave your hands above your head, and move away. Almost all people injured by bears in the Smokies have been feeding them.

# WHERE TO FIND WILDFLOWERS

Below are some suggestions of good places to find wildflowers in season. The suggestions have been divided into three categories: hikes, walks, and drives. Hikes are trails of more than a couple of miles that will get you out into a variety of habitats with the potential for numerous species to be seen. *Hiking Trails of the Smokies* can be used to get an in-depth description of each hike. Walks are strolls of a mile or less which will give you the opportunity to see a number of different wildflowers in a short time. And finally, drives are along slow paced roads, some of which offer exceptional wildflower watching potential.

The most up-to-date information about wildflowers can be found by inquiring at one of the three visitor centers in the park (Sugarlands, Oconaluftee and Cades Cove). You can help keep other wildflower watchers up-to-date by providing the rangers with current blooming reports of your hikes, walks, and drives. A simple blooming report consists of the common names of all flowers seen on a trail or road. Scientific names can be added to help avoid confusion. And special notes of unusual sightings can make a blooming report helpful to park botanists in their research.

**HIKES**—In early spring, March through April, three trails stand out for their plant diversity. On the North Carolina side of the park is Bradley Fork Trail, starting from D-Loop in Smokemont Campground. In Tennessee, Porters Creek Trail in Greenbrier and the Chestnut Top Trail near Townsend are exceptional.

Bradley Fork starts as an old road following the creek of the same name. The trail stays relatively low for the first few miles rising at only a moderate pace. After about five miles, the trail begins to climb more steeply, going from 3,500 feet to over 5,000 feet in just over two miles. The lower end of this trail abounds in wildflowers early in the season. Hepatica, violets, foamflower and other rich woods species can be seen here. Later on in the season, these plants can be found up higher on the trail along with umbrella leaf and Fraser's sedge. In the summer, bee-balm and jewelweed spot the trail. Although nearly 7.3 miles long, it will hold your attention all along the way.

Porters Creek Trail starts at the end of the Greenbrier Road 5.9 miles east of Gatlinburg. Like its North Carolina counterpart, this trail begins as an old road. After about one mile, it enters a thick hardwood forest and narrows into a single foot path. You can expect to find everything from bloodroot to painted trillium along this trail. Up near Fern Branch Falls (1.9 miles) is a spectacular display of fringed phacelia. The trail climbs gradually over its entire 3.7 miles, ending at campsite #31, just over 3,500 feet in elevation.

Chestnut Top Trail could be considered either a hike or a walk; although it is 4.3 miles long, it is the first 0.5 mile which contains the most of wildflowers. Starting just inside the park from the Townsend entrance, the trail climbs along a hillside paralleling the road and Little River. Seeps on the hillside keep the area moist, providing habitat for sweet white trillium, Jack-in-the-pulpit, bishop's cap and the purple phacelia. Drier slopes also provide the appropriate growing conditions for fire pink and plantain-leaved pussytoes. After the first half mile, the trail levels out and climbs slowly through pine-oak forests to Schoolhouse Gap, a bit over three miles away. Although not as bountiful, the scattered wildflowers are still worth the journey.

Sometimes a nice loop can be created by combining a couple of trails. A good early spring loop hike is in the Elkmont area. Start on Jakes Creek Trail, 1.1 miles above Elkmont Campground (stay to the right after the campground). Follow this old railroad bed just 0.3 mile before turning left onto Cucumber Gap Trail. This short trail (2.3 miles) starts and ends at nearly the same elevation, climbing and descending at similar slopes about 500 feet to and from Cucumber Gap. When it reaches the Little River Trail turn left again and descend back to the Elkmont area. This old railroad bed will gently descend along the Little River about two miles before reaching the road junction you took to the right to get to the Jakes Creek Trailhead. Turn left again to reach your car about half a mile away. Along the way you will be dazzled with a profusion of spring color. Trilliums, hepatica, violets, spring-beauties and the like abound here.

**WALKS**—As mentioned above, a good spring walk is along the Chestnut Top Trail at the Townsend "Y" (intersection of Highway 73, Little River Road and Laurel Creek Road). The first half mile of this trail is a wildflower watcher's dream come true. As many as 40 species, including the unusual sweet white trillium, can be seen here at the peak of spring color. This trail is rivaled by only two others for exceptional spring color in such a short distance—the Cosby and Cove Hardwood Self-guiding Nature Trails.

The Cosby Nature Trail is located at the Cosby Campground. This one mile trail jumps in and out of numerous forest types creating a virtual tapestry of color. Old homesites along the way provide small openings for the lovely Vasey's trillium. Deep, rich soils also give squirrel corn and Dutchman's britches a place to grow. Brook lettuce can be found in Cosby Creek and squawroot can be seen poking up from beneath the forest litter. This trail at the far eastern end of the park is a bit off the beaten track which allows it to remain quiet and peaceful when others are over-crowded.

Six miles south of Gatlinburg on the Newfound Gap Road, starting within the Chimneys Picnic Area, is the Cove Hardwood Nature Trail. It is a magnificent walk. Starting in an old farming area, the trail climbs a small hillside into old growth forests before returning you to your car. As you climb through the forest your senses will come alive with the sights, sounds, and smells of spring. Solomon's seal shares the area with wild ginger. Trout-lilies and white trilliums splash their color everywhere. Even the little things excel here. The display of the tiny fringed phacelia will make you think of a spring snowfall for they completely cover the ground with white blossoms.

In the species descriptions, you will also see reference to another short walk, the Schoolhouse Gap Trail just east of Cades Cove. This trail offers you the opportunity to observe some unusual species. Southern harebell, cardinal flower, and fairy wand can be found here at different times of the year.

**DRIVES**—Although every road in the park offers the observant driver a diversity of wildflowers, we will focus on just three here. The Balsam Mountain Road, Roaring Fork Motor Nature Trail, and Rich Mountain roads are all low speed, less-traveled byways offering outstanding wildflower opportunities. A word of caution for travel on a road is to be aware of your surroundings. All these roads have many curves. The park rangers respond every year to numerous single-car accidents, the result of a simple lack of concentration on the road. Also, please remember to be a courteous driver and allow faster traffic to pass you by. Pullouts along these roads will also give you the opportunity to walk back and better observe unusual plants you see along the way.

The Balsam Mountain Road in North Carolina starts near the Balsam Mountain Campground. This road begins as a one-way gravel road at Heintooga Overlook and Picnic Area and winds down along the slopes of Cataloochee Balsam and Chiltoes Mountains to the Straight Fork River at Round Bottom. Here the road widens into a two-way gravel drive. The fact that this road drops from more than 5,000 feet to less than 3,000 feet provides a diversity of wildflowers. This is a nice summer drive at which time you will find coneflower, bee-balm, and monk's hood amongst the numerous blossoms dotting the road. You can reach this road by taking the Blue Ridge Parkway which starts just south of Oconaluftee Visitor Center near Cherokee, North Carolina. Turn north onto the Heintooga Ridge Road, which becomes the Balsam Mountain Road past the campground entrance. Plan on taking at least two to three hours to visit this area. A full day would be necessary to do it justice, however.

If you find yourself on the main parkway in Gatlinburg, turn onto Airport Road at stop light #8 to find a marvelous drive called, appropriately, Roaring Fork Motor Nature Trail. Like Balsam Mountain Road, you should plan on spending at least a couple of hours here, but a full day would be a better plan. This winding, one-way paved road starts at the end of Cherokee Orchard Road near the trailhead to Rainbow Falls. It meanders its way across a small ridge and then down along Roaring Fork before leading back into the rush of Gatlinburg. Of the three roads discussed here, this will have the heaviest traffic, but on a nice spring day, it is well worth any amount of traffic. Here you will find an abundance of species of rich woods, like smooth Solomon's seal and blue phlox. Numerous trails leave this road and can be explored for short or long distances.

Finally, the Rich Mountain Road is a six mile one-way gravel road taking you from Cades Cove over Rich Gap to the park boundary and a two-way paved road leading into Townsend. This road mostly traverses dry hillsides where flowers like bird's foot violet and bowman's root can be found. Yet it also passes into deep rich coves where large-flowered bellwort and Indian-pink bloom. You will find this road to be relatively quiet even during the peak of wildflowers in April and May.

# WHAT TO LOOK FOR IN A WILDFLOWER

You don't need to be a professional botanist to identify wild-flowers. However, you do need to be observant of details and learn some basic plant parts. Botanists have technical terms for all parts of a plant, but we have tried to avoid using these terms in this book. Instead, we have tried to use every-day language to describe flower parts, leaf characters, and habitat descriptions. In addition, we have included a glossary to assist you.

To help you identify your U.F.O. (Unidentified Flowering Object), it is important to note not only the flower color, but other characters of the plant as well. Here's a short list of some of the characteristics you might note:

1. HABITAT: sun/shade; wet/dry; open area/woodland; elevation
2. FLOWER: color; number of petals; number of flower heads per plant
3. LEAF PATTERN: opposite or alternate; no leaves; basal only
4. LEAF SHAPE: toothed, lobed, untoothed, divided

## BASICS OF WILDFLOWER IDENTIFICATION . . . . .

Try not to focus solely on the blossom when identifying a wildflower: the stem, leaves, roots, and habitat may give significant clues. Also, try to look at several individual plants before attempting identification. Just as humans vary from individual to individual, no single wildflower will be "typical" of its species. While we have tried to emphasize features of the wildflower that are easily seen, a ruler and a hand lens may be useful.

The blossom is the reproductive organ of a wildflower. Unisexual flowers are either male (produce only pollen) or female (produce only seed). Most flowers are "perfect," that is, have both male and female organs. The female pistil contains both the pollen-receiving organ (stigma) and the seed-producing organ (ovary). The male organs are stamens. They are usually stalked and have pollen-producing sacs (anthers) at the tips. In most flowers, petals and sepals surround the sexual organs. The petals (collectively known as corolla) are often large and brightly colored. The sepals (together called the calyx) are usually green or brown and somewhat leafy. The number, size, and shape of both petals and sepals can be important identification characters.

Flowers can grow in different arrangements on a plant — solitary, in clusters, in heads, etc. A "spike" is an elongated cluster of flowers. An "umbel" is a flat or rounded broad cluster. A "head" is a flower cluster so dense that it appears to be a single flower. The Aster family uses flower heads in a particularly efficient manner so that dozens or hundreds of very tiny flowers are packed into a small space. A sunflower, for example, is not a single flower, but hundreds of tiny disk flowers (the "eye") surrounded by dozens of ray flowers which people often mistake for petals.

Flowers can grow on different parts of the plant: at the top of the stalk ("terminal"), from the joint between the leaf and the stem ("axial"), or even on the ground ("basal").

Leaves are important identification features. Leaves growing from the base of the plant are "basal," those growing above the base are stem leaves. Some plants have both basal and stem leaves, others have one or the other, while some plants, when they flower, have no leaves at all. A cluster of basal leaves is called a "rosette." When stem leaves grow in pairs they are "opposite" on the stem. When more than two leaves grow in a circle around the stem they are "whorled." Leaves that grow singly on the stem, alternating from one side to the other, are called "alternate."

Leaf pattern is also a useful identification feature. If a leaf has a smooth, unbroken edge it is "entire." A leaf with indented edges is "toothed," "scalloped," or "serrate," depending on the number and sharpness of the indentations. Indentations that are very deep result in "lobes." An example of a lobed leaf would be a maple leaf. Sometimes the leaf is actually "divided" into leaflets. An example of a divided leaf is clover (three leaflets).

Habitat is often overlooked as an aid to identification. Moisture and drainage, degree of shade, elevation, and surrounding vegetation all play a role in plant survival. Make special note of the "elevation range" and "habitat" information when using this guide. If you are hiking on a woodland trail around the Sugarlands Visitor Center and tentatively identify a plant as Rugel's ragwort, look again! Rugel's ragwort is a rare plant that grows in the moist understory of high elevation forests.

# WILDFLOWER ACTIVITIES . . . . . . . . . . . . . . . .

Learning to identify wildflowers is just one way to enjoying the native flora of Great Smoky Mountains National Park. Wildflower photography, learning about folk and medicinal uses of wild plants, arts and crafts using natural materials, natural history writing, and growing native plants in home gardens are just some of the activities that wildflower enthusiasts enjoy.

One of the most popular wildflower activities takes place in the park in late April every year. The Spring Wildflower Pilgrimage is a three-day program of guided nature walks, motorcades and photographic tours in the Great Smoky Mountains National Park. Sponsors are the Botany Department of The University of Tennessee, the Gatlinburg Garden Club, the Southern Appalachian Botanical Society, Great Smoky Mountains Association, and Great Smoky Mountains National Park. The pilgrimage is one of the very best ways to learn the trails and plants of the park.

Many visitors enjoy photographing the plants of the park. When taking a photograph, please be sure that you do not damage the plant or the plants growing around it. Never pick or damage plants in the park. To get unwanted plants out of the photograph, gently bend them behind other plants, then restore them once you are done. Careful placement of feet (yours and your tripod's) is essential to ensure the safety of small seedlings and other delicate plants.

Native Americans and early settlers to the Smoky Mountains relied on plants for their food, medicines, and craft materials. Park naturalists are well versed not only in the plants and animals of the Smokies, but also in the human history of the area. Programs highlighting the lives of the people who lived in the park are offered during the warmer months.

Many writers have been inspired by the beauty of the Smoky Mountains. Park visitor centers offer a wide selection of books about the plants, animals, geology, hiking, and people of the Smokies. Such books are also available by mail order. Contact Great Smoky Mountains Association, 115 Park Headquarters Road, Gatlinburg, TN 37738 (865) 436-0120.

Native wildflowers can make wonderful garden plants, and an increasing number of nurseries offer native plants. Please remember that all plants in the park are protected, and they cannot be dug or collected. "Conservation through Propagation" is central to protecting the native flora of the Smoky Mountains. Propagation means that you start a new plant by collecting seed. Instead of digging a plant from the wild, reputable nursery growers will collect seeds and propagate the plants. By using only nursery-propagated plants, we conserve the original plant in its natural setting and enjoy its offspring in our yards. To obtain information on nurseries that offer seed or propagated plants, contact the North Carolina Botanical Garden, CB# 3375, University of North Carolina, Chapel Hill, NC 27599-3375 (phone 919-962-0522).

## GUIDEBOOKS AND REFERENCES . . . . . . . . . . .

No single book can cover everything there is to see in the Great Smoky Mountains National Park. The visitor centers in the park carry a wide range of books about the human and natural history of the park and its surroundings.

If your particular interest is in plants, you may want to refer to more books to help you identify wildflowers, vines, shrubs, trees, and ferns not found in this book.

While there are several technical manuals for identification of plants in the southeastern United States, there is a paucity of field guides for the region in the popular press. The Great Smoky Mountains pose a particular challenge since the plant diversity is so high: Clingmans Dome harbors plant species common in New England, while lower elevations have plants typical to Georgia and South Carolina. Many plants are found in only the southeastern United States, and some are restricted to only a small area in and around the Great Smoky Mountains. You may need to consult several books—perhaps even delve into technical manuals—to identify some plants!

Here is a list of some books that may help you learn more about the vegetation of the Great Smoky Mountains.

Bolyard, J.L. (1981) *Medicinal Plants and Home Remedies of Appalachia*. Charles C. Thomas Publisher, Springfield, IL.

Hamel, Paul B. and Chiltoskey, Mary U. (1975) *Cherokee Plants and Their Uses — a 400 year history*. Herald Publishing Company, Sylva, NC. —Medicinal and folk uses of plants of the Appalachian Mountains.

Houk, Rose (1993) *Great Smoky Mountains National Park: A Natural History Guide*. Houghton Mifflin Company, Boston. —Human and natural history of the park.

Kemp, Steve (1993) *Trees of the Smokies*. Great Smoky Mountains Association, Gatlinburg, TN —color photos and key cover trees and conspicuous shrubs of the park.

Lellinger, David B. (1985) *A Field Manual of the Ferns and Fern-Allies of the United States and Canada*. Smithsonian Institution Press, Washington, DC. —Technical key of wide coverage.

Newcomb, Lawrence (1977) *Newcomb's Wildflower Guide*. Little, Brown and Company, Boston, MA. —Range of coverage is from Nova Scotia through Virginia, but includes many plants found in park. Does not have southern Appalachian endemics, but does have vines and shrubs.

Radford, Albert E., Ahles, Harry E., and Bell, C. Ritchie (1964) *Manual of the Vascular Flora of the Carolinas*. The University of North Carolina Press, Chapel Hill, NC. —The "bible" for botanists of the southeast United States. Technical, includes ferns, grasses, wildflowers and woody plants.

Sharp, A.J., Wofford, E., and White, P. "Keys and Checklist to the Common Spring Wildflowers of the Great Smoky Mountains National Park" —A technical key to spring wildflowers.

Stupka, Arthur (1964) *Trees, Shrubs and Woody Vines of Great Smoky Mountains National Park*. University of Tennessee Press, Knoxville, TN. —Excellent reference on the woody plants of the park.

Great Smoky Mountains Association (1982) "Flowering Plants of the Great Smoky Mountains" —A checklist for all flowering plants in the park, can be purchased at park visitor centers.

White, Peter S. (1982) "The flora of Great Smoky Mountain National park: an annotated checklist of the vascular plants and a review of previous floristic work." USDI, National Park Service, Southeast Regional Office, Research/Resource Manage. Rept. SER-55. 219 pg. —A comprehensive study of the vegetation of the park.

Wofford, B. Eugene (1989) *Guide to the Vascular Plants of the Blue Ridge*. The University of Georgia Press, Athens, GA. —Technical key includes ferns, grasses, wildflowers and woody plants.

Many of these publication are available at park visitor centers or by contacting Great Smoky Mountains Association, 115 Park Headquarters Road, Gatlinburg, TN 37738 (865) 436-0120. www.SmokiesStore.org.

# INCLUDED/EXCLUDED SPECIES

This book presents the native wildflowers of the park. The native species are the ones that so characterize the distinctive environments, geography, and history of the Smokies. In emphasizing native species, this book highlights what is most distinctive about the Smokies. In addition, we want to encourage you to explore the park's natural habitats and to understand the relation between wildflowers and those habitats.

In contrast to "native," ecologists use "exotic," "alien," or "non-native" to describe plants brought purposefully or accidentally by people. Not only are these species not part of the distinctive biological diversity that the park protects, they sometimes are pests that displace native species. None, therefore, have been included in the main identification section of this guide.

Most exotic plants occur in areas disturbed by people. The dandelion of roadsides and lawns is a perfect example. European settlers originally brought dandelions to North America as a vegetable plant—for salads—but it soon escaped the confines of garden walls.

While some exotic plants, like the dandelion and mullein, reproduce by seed in the park, others like daffodils are almost always found near old homesites. They persist there, and spread vegetatively, but rarely reproduce by seed. These are not considered the threat to the park that aggressive species such as kudzu, Japanese grass, and Oriental bittersweet are. Even though several hundred exotic plant species are now found in the park, only about 25 are considered pests in the sense that they invade natural habitats and displace native species.

Exotic wildflowers are usually plants of low elevation fields, lawns, and roadsides, rather than plants of the park's wild places. While they may be conspicuous as you drive the park's roads, almost all of them have vanished by the time you enter the deep woods.

The list below is of the common exotic wildflowers. We annotate the ones that may be seen away from the park's roads.

## Common Exotic Wildflowers in the Great Smokies

| COMMON NAME | SCIENTIFIC NAMES | NOTES |
|---|---|---|
| Yarrow | *Achillea millefolium* | Grassy balds |
| Field garlic | *Allium vineale* | |
| Wintercress | *Barbarea vulgaris* | |
| Bittercress | *Cardamine hirsuta* | |
| Mouse-ear chickweed | *Cerastium holosteoides* | Trailsides |
| Ox-eye daisy | *Leucanthemum vulgare* | Trailsides |
| Queen Ann's Lace | *Daucus carota* | Openings |
| Gill-over-the-ground | *Glechoma hederacea* | Trailsides |
| Yellow hawkweed | *Hieracium pratense* | Openings |
| St. John's-wort | *Hypericum perforatum* | |
| Morning-glory | *Ipomoea hederacea* | |
| Purple morning-glory | *Ipomoea purpurea* | |
| Henbit | *Lamium amplexicaule* | |
| Purple dead-nettle | *Lamium purpureum* | |
| Daffodil | *Narcissus pseudo-narcissus* | Homesites |
| Wild parsnip | *Pastinaca sativa* | |
| Rough-fruited cinquefoil | *Potentilla recta* | |
| Tall buttercup | *Ranunculus acris* | Wet thickets |
| Basil | *Satureja vulgaris* | |
| Common chickweed | *Stellaria media* | |
| Dandelion | *Taraxacum officinale* | Openings |
| Alsike clover | *Trifolium hybridum* | Openings |
| Red clover | *Trifolium pratense* | Openings |
| White clover | *Trifolium repens* | Openings |
| Mullein | *Verbascum thaspus* | |
| Speedwell | *Veronica officinalis* | Trailsides |
| Periwinkle | *Vinca minor* | Homesites |
| Wild pansy | *Viola rafinesquii* | Moist thickets |

Herbaceous, rather than woody, plants are emphasized in this book. Botanists distinguish woody from herbaceous species with the following definitions: woody plants are perennial and above ground in the winter (their woody tissues have buds that renew growth from the above ground parts in the spring), whereas herbaceous plants are either annuals (which go to seed each year), biennials (which go to seed in alternate years and often spend the intervening winter as a basal rosette of leaves at the ground surface), or perennials (which are dormant below ground in the winter). Woody plants include trees, shrubs, and woody vines.

For more information on woody plants, many of which have beautiful flowers, see *Trees of the Smokies* by Steve Kemp or *Trees, Shrubs, and Woody Vines of Great Smoky Mountains National Park* by Arthur Stupka. To purchase a copy, stop by a park visitor center or call (865) 436-0120. www.SmokiesStore.org.

# How to Use This Book

This book describes over 250 species of native wildflowers that a visitor may encounter along the roadsides and trails of the park. The plants are arranged first by flower color:

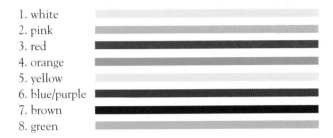

1. white
2. pink
3. red
4. orange
5. yellow
6. blue/purple
7. brown
8. green

Within color they are arranged so that similar looking species are grouped together:

- simple flowers (such as violets)
- daisy-like flowers
- irregularly-shaped flowers (such as lady's slipper orchids)
- upright spikes (such as galax, foam flower, etc.)
- flat or rounded clusters (such as goldenrod, New York ironweed, etc.)
- vines.

Most of the information on the species' identification pages is self-explanatory with the exception of the elevation, abundance, and location "call-outs" (see chart on following pages).

Blooming time (BLOOMS) refers to the most common months of flowering. During certain years, and on certain sites, you may find flowers blooming earlier or later than stated.

## ELEVATION

Where this species grows.
**low elevation** = 800-2,500
**mid elevation** = 2,500-4,500
**high elevation** = 4,500-6,643
**wide range** = occurs at all elevations

## ABUNDANCE

How common the plant is in Great Smoky Mountains
National Park.
**Common**—Plant is characteristic of the Smokies and
dominant here.
**Frequent**—Plant is generally encountered here.
**Occasional**—Plant is well distributed, but nowhere
abundant.
**Infrequent**—Plant can be found in scattered locations
throughout the park.
**Scarce**—Plant can be found in several locations or
scattered, small populations.
**Rare**—Plant is found in only one or two locations in the
park.

## LOCATION

In most cases we have listed a road or trail where this plant can
be viewed in season. This does not mean these locations are
the only places in the park where they can be seen. In a few
cases, where plant poaching is a concern, or no reliable location has been documented, no locations are provided.

*Trillium grandiflorum*

# WHITE TRILLIUM

Lily Family
(Liliaceae)

Plant: 8"-18"
(20-46 cm)
Flower: 2"-4"
(5-10 cm)

Low-mid elevation
Common

One of the showiest of the trilliums, white trillium's huge single flower stands on a stalk above the whorl of the three leaves characteristic of the trilliums. The flower's three large petals with wavy edges are usually white but turn various shades of pink as the flower fades with age. This color change signals to insects and other pollinators that pollination has already occurred.

Native Americans chewed the rhizomes of this species to ward off the effects of snakebite. In 1934, a botanist celebrated the dedication of the national park by writing that the trilliums were at last safe from feral pigs. Little did he know that by 1950 European wild hogs would permanently establish themselves in the Smokies.

◆ **HABITAT**—Moist woods, coves.
◆ **LOCATION**—Newfound Gap Road, Cove Hardwood Nature Trail
◆ **BLOOMS APRIL - MAY**

72

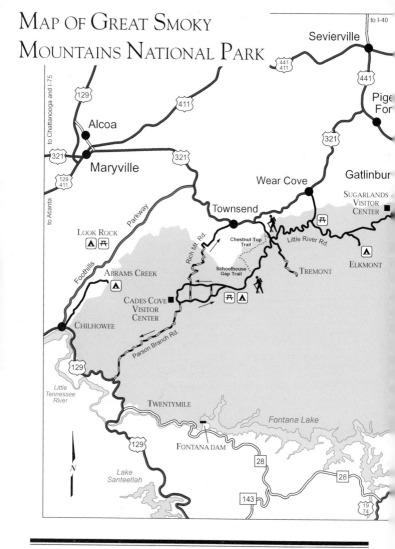

# MAP OF GREAT SMOKY MOUNTAINS NATIONAL PARK

Sevierville

to I-40

441
411

441

Pige
For

129

411

to Chattanooga and I-75

Alcoa

321

321

Maryville

321

Wear Cove

Gatlinbur

SUGARLANDS
VISITOR
CENTER

Townsend

129
411

to Atlanta

Parkway

LOOK ROCK

Rich Mt. Rd.

Chestnut Top
Trail

Little River Rd.

ELKMONT

TREMONT

Foothills

ABRAMS CREEK

Schoolhouse
Gap Trail

CADES COVE
VISITOR
CENTER

CHILHOWEE

129

Parson Branch Rd.

Little
Tennessee
River

TWENTYMILE

Fontana Lake

FONTANA DAM

28

129

N

28

Lake
Santeetlah

143

19
74

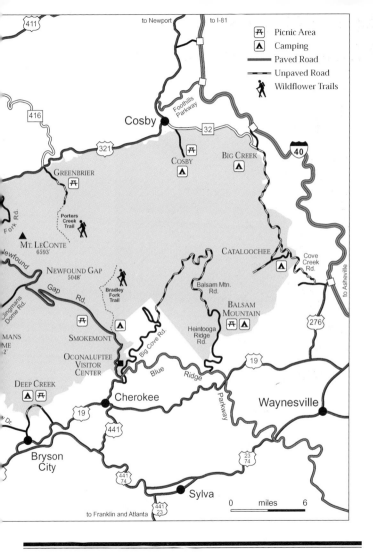

# TRAILING ARBUTUS

*Epigaea repens*

Heath Family
(*Ericaceae*)

Plant: low woody
shrub
Flower: ½″
(1.3 cm)

Wide range
Common

Joseph G. Strauch, Jr.

As old man winter begins to release his icy grip on the Smokies, look for this little flower. The small tubular blossom may be hidden beneath leaf litter. Its sweet-spicy scent could lead your nose to it before your eyes. The leaves you see now are last year's. The plant gets a jump on the growing season by keeping its old leaves. Only after the flowers fade will new leaves grow to collect energy for next year.

This is the earliest flowering wildflower in the Smokies. Over-collecting by the florist industry in the early 1900s nearly made it extinct. It is also known as mayflower. Legend holds that it was the first flower seen by the Pilgrims after their disastrous first winter in New England.

♦ **HABITAT**—Dry, pine-oak forests, heath balds, trailsides.
♦ **LOCATIONS**—Rich Mountain Road, Little River Trail.
♦ **BLOOMS MARCH - MAY**

*Hepatica nobilis*
var. *acuta*

Buttercup Family
(*Ranunculaceae*)

Plant: 3"-6"
(8-15 cm)
Flower: ½"-1"
(1.3-2.5 cm)

Low-mid elevation
Frequent

Bill Lea

Hepatica blooms as early as February and is gone from the mountains by late April. Warm sunlight falling through the still-leafless forest canopy gives hepatica a jump on the season.

The single flower sits atop a short hairy stalk. It has 5-9 white, sometimes pink or blue, sepals. Below sits a cluster of dark, three-lobed leaves. As the common name implies, this hepatica's leaves come to a sharp point. When the pollinated flower matures into seeds, hepatica's main stalk lengthens and droops to near the ground. Ants then collect and disperse the seeds.

Mountain folklore tells farmers to get ready for planting when hepatica appears.

◆ **HABITAT**— Rich woods.
◆ **LOCATIONS**—Cove Hardwood Nature Trail, Tremont Road.
◆ **BLOOMS MARCH - APRIL**

# WOOD ANEMONE

*Anemone quinquefolia*

Buttercup Family
(*Ranunculaceae*)

Plant: 4"-10"
(10-25 cm)
Flower: 1"
(2.5 cm)

Wide range
Frequent

Jessie M. Harris

There are many unusual things about this plant. For one, its flower has no petals. The 5-15 white (rarely pink or blue) structures are actually sepals. The solitary bloom also has very little nectar to attract pollinators. It produces an over-abundance of pollen, however. Early botanists thought this was for wind pollination, but bees knew better. Pollen is as valuable a food for insects as nectar.

The whorl of three leaves, with their three sharply-lobed leaflets, may leave you asking why *quinquefolia*? The "five leaves" refers to the basal leaves which tend to be five segmented. Because it freely waves in the wind, it has been called windflower.

◆ **HABITAT**—Rich woods.

◆ **LOCATIONS**—Laurel Creek Road, Bradley Fork Trail.

◆ **BLOOMS APRIL - MAY**

Buttercup Family
(*Ranunculaceae*)

Plant: 4″-8″
(10-20 cm)
Flower: ¾″-1″
(1.9-2.5 cm)

Low-mid elevation
Frequent

*leaves*

Ed Ponikwia

Rue-Anemone has 1-5 (usually three) white blossoms. The similar wood anemone (*Anemone quinquefolia*) has a solitary flower and very different leaves. Both species have similar flowers composed of 5-10 white sepals surrounding a cluster of pistils and stamens. Rue-anemone leaves resemble meadow rue (*Thalictrum dioicum*) leaves; they are compound with lobed leaflets.

In ancient times, Persians considered a similar species so poisonous it could foul the air. They often held their breath when passing this plant. There is no need to fear observing the blossoms, but be careful if you handle the plant. The sap was once used to burn the corns off feet.

◆ **HABITAT**—Rich woods.
◆ **LOCATIONS**—Newfound Gap Road, Bradley Fork Trail.
◆ **BLOOMS APRIL - MAY**

# STAR CHICKWEED

*Stellaria pubera*

Pink Family
*(Caryophyllaceae)*

Plant: 6"-12"
(15-30 cm)
Flower: ⅓"-½"
(0.8-1.3 cm)

Low-mid elevation
Common

Jessie M. Harris

*petals & sepals
of star chickweed*

What may appear as 10 petals are really just five. Each petal is cut almost to its base giving a false impression. Divided petals are characteristic of the pink family. The flower has dark, globular anthers giving it a delicate look. It is sometimes called great chickweed because of its large, showy flowers (large by chickweed standards, anyway). The stem is marked with a row of tiny hairs which alternate sides at each node. The closely related Core's chickweed (*S. corei*) has sepals longer than its petals and the upper leaves often have short stems.

Mountain folklore says that an open chickweed flower guarantees a few hours without rain. Birds forage eagerly for this plant's seeds, hence the common name "chickweed."

◆ **HABITAT**—Moist woods.

◆ **LOCATIONS**—Chestnut Top Trail, Laurel Creek Road.

◆ **BLOOMS APRIL - MAY**

*Sanguinaria canadensis*

# BLOODROOT

Poppy family
(*Papaveraceae*)

Plant: up to 10″
(25 cm)
Flower: to 1½″
(3.8 cm)

Low elevation
Frequent

*seed capsule*

Jessie M. Harris

The fragile bloodroot is one of the first wildflowers to bloom each year, its single flower appearing well before the trees leaf out. Notice the narrow white petals surrounding a center of many golden stamens and the single pistil. The distinctively veiny and deeply-lobed leaf may be from 4″-7″ across. Each flower is short lived and is replaced by a double-pointed capsule containing the seeds.

The orangish-red juice found in the rhizome inspired both the common and generic name, which is Latin for "bleeding." The Cherokee and other Native Americans used bloodroot extensively as a dye for baskets and clothing, as well as for body paint. In large quantities the juice is poisonous and can be lethal.

◆ **HABITAT**—Moist woods, flood plains.
◆ **LOCATIONS**—Porters Creek Trail, Rich Mountain Road.
◆ **BLOOMS MARCH-APRIL**

# CANADIAN VIOLET

*Viola canadensis*

Violet Family
(*Violaceae*)

Plant: 8"-16"
(20-41 cm)
Flower: ¾"-1 ¼"
(1.8-2.8 cm)

Wide range
Frequent

Harry Ellis

Violets can be easily separated into two groups: those with above ground stems bearing both leaves and flowers, and those with no above ground stem, leaves in a rosette, and single flowers on a leafless stalk. The Canadian violet is a stemmed violet and easy to recognize by its tall stature. The leaves are heart-shaped. The white flowers have purple veins on the lower three petals and a purple tinge on the back of the uppermost petals. The flower fades to purple with age.

There are two varieties of *canadensis* in the Great Smokies: one that forms dense colonies by way of underground branches called stolons, and the other without this mode of reproduction. Both varieties are common in the park's moist woodlands.

◆ **HABITAT**—Moist, rich woods and rocky slopes.
◆ **LOCATIONS**—Little River Road, Bradley Fork Trail.
◆ **BLOOMS APRIL - JULY**

# NORTHERN WHITE VIOLET

*Viola
macloskeyi* ssp.
*pallens*

Violet Family
*(Violaceae)*

Plant: 6″
(15 cm)
Flower: ¼″-½″
(0.6-1.3 cm)

Mid-high elevation
Frequent

Ken Voorhis

There are two groups of violets: those with several leaves alternating along an above ground stem (the stemmed violets) and those with no above ground stem and leaves on petioles (stalks) arranged in a rosette. This stemless violet has small rounded leaves and a tiny white fragrant flower. It can be confused with the similar sweet white violet *(V. blanda)*, which has a larger flower and two upper petals that are twisted backward. The northern white violet has hairless leaves while the sweet white violet has tiny hairs visible with a hand lens. Their habitats are also different, the sweet white violet prefers rich forests at low to mid elevations.

◆ **HABITAT**— Streamsides, seeps, and cool shaded woods.
◆ **LOCATION**—Balsam Mountain/Heintooga Ridge roads, The Boulevard Trail.
◆ **BLOOMS APRIL - MAY**

# CUT-LEAVED TOOTHWORT

Jessie M. Harris

*Cardamine concatenata*

Mustard Family
(*Brassicaceae*)

Plant: 8″-10″
(20-25 cm)
Flower: ¾″
(1.9 cm)

Low-mid elevation
Frequent

A cluster of tiny white (rarely pink) cross-shaped flowers sits atop a three-leaved stalk. Inside, six stamens await flying insects needed to transfer their pollen. After pollination, an inch-long pod called a silique develops. This ultra-thin fruit splits along a central membrane casting its minute seeds to the wind.

A whorl of three deeply cut and toothed leaves are on the upper half of the stem while in flower. Later, basal leaves will develop. These add energy to the segmented rhizome below. The shape of the rhizome is responsible for the toothwort name. Cresses, as mountain farmers called it, was a favorite spring herb. Leaves were smothered in bacon grease or soaked in vinegar. The peppery root was nibbled in the field.

◆ **HABITAT**—Rich woods.

◆ **LOCATIONS**—Rich Mountain Road, Kanati Fork Trail.

◆ **BLOOMS  APRIL - MAY**

## *Cardamine diphylla*

Mustard Family
(*Brassicaceae*)

Plant: 8"-12"
(20-30 cm)
Flower: ½"-1"
(1.3-2.5 cm)

Wide range
Common

Joseph G. Strauch, Jr.

Like the cut-leaved toothwort (*C. concatenata*), toothwort also has a cluster of white flowers at its apex. However, toothwort has a pair of three-parted leaves below the flower cluster. The leaves are opposite or nearly so on the stem. The three divisions of the basal leaves are more elliptic than those on the stem. Toothworts, like other members of the Mustard family, have four petals, four sepals, and six stamens.

Toothworts were highly prized by mountain people because of the strong, radish-like, peppery taste of their rhizome. Ancient physicians erroneously thought the tooth-like projections on the white rhizome of this plant meant that it could cure a toothache.

♦ **HABITAT**—Rich woods.
♦ **LOCATIONS**—Newfound Gap Road, Porters Creek Trail.
♦ **BLOOMS APRIL - MAY**

# SWEET CICELY

*Osmorhiza claytonii*

Parsley Family
(Apiaceae)

Plant: 1'-2'
(4-8 dm)
Flower: Umbellets
¼"-½"
Umbels 1"-2"
(20-50 mm)

Low-mid elevation
O. *claytoni*:
common;
O. *longistylis*:
frequent

Jessie M. Harris

It's easy to distinguish sweet cicely from its close relative, long-styled anise root (*Osmorhiza longistylis*) by the smell of their foliage and roots: sweet cicely has a bland odor, while anise root has a strong anise (licorice) odor. Both are perennials. The foliage is reminiscent of parsley—dissected leaves and coarsely serrated edges. The inflorescence is a compound umbel. With a hand lens, look for a minute flower with white petals. Note that each minute flower is part of a small cluster (umbellet) of flowers. Several umbellets radiate from a common stem and form a larger group of flowers, a compound umbel. A single plant may have several compound umbels, and therefore hundreds of minute flowers. Other famous members of the Parsley family include carrot, dill, celery, and the deadly water hemlock.

◆ **HABITAT**—Moist fertile forests.
◆ **BLOOMS APRIL ∙ MAY**

# GRASS-OF-PARNASSUS

*Parnassia
asarifolia*

Saxifrage Family
(*Saxifragaceae*)

Plant: 4″-18″
(1-5 dm)
Flower: 1″-1¼″
(3-11 cm)

Mid-high elevation
Rare

Jessie M. Harris

Consider yourself very lucky to find this outstanding native of bogs
and seepage slopes. The leaves are basal, smooth-edged, thick in texture, and kidney-shaped. The shape of these leaves is reminiscent of
deciduous wild ginger, *Asarum*, hence the species name, *asarifolia*. Each
flower has 5 stamens (pollen-producing organs). Each flower also has 5
staminodia (sterile stamens), each deeply 3-lobed to base, thus appearing as 15. The staminodia are slightly shorter than the stamens.

Appalachian grass-of-parnassus is found in mountainous highlands
of the Appalachian Mountains in the southeastern United States, and
westward into the Ozark Mountains of Arkansas and Texas. The genus
is named for Mount Parnassus in Greece, a place sacred to the Muses.

◆ **HABITAT**—Bogs, seepage slopes, streambanks.
◆ **LOCATION**—Alum Cave Trail.
◆ **BLOOMS AUGUST - OCTOBER**

69

# MAY-APPLE

*Podophyllum peltatum*

Barberry Family
(*Berberidaceae*)

Plant: 12"-18"
(30-46 cm)
Flower: 1"-2"
(2.5-5 cm)

Wide range
Common

Connie Toops

This perennial is commonly found growing in large groups. Its umbrella-like leaves stand upright. On two-leaved plants, look below the leaves to see a solitary white flower. The large flower with its waxy petals nods on a short stalk growing from the notch between the two leaves. In summer, may-apple sports yellow, egg-shaped, edible berries.

May-apple was used by the Cherokee for many ailments, including liver troubles, warts, and to restore hearing. Modern medical research has discovered anti-cancer properties and it is being used actively against lung and breast cancer. The apple-shaped berries were made into jellies by mountain families. Be warned, though, large dosages can be toxic and potentially deadly.

- ◆ **HABITAT**—Moist, hardwood forests.
- ◆ **LOCATIONS**—Little River Road, Porters Creek Trail.
- ◆ **BLOOMS APRIL - JUNE**

# WILD STRAWBERRY

*Fragaria virginiana*

Rose Family
(*Rosaceae*)

Plant: 3"-6"
(8-15 cm)
Flower: ½"-¾"
(1.3-1.9 cm)

Wide Range
Frequent

*"strawberry"*

Tom Barnes

This low-growing plant with its small white flowers might get overlooked in spring, but it is highly sought after in summer when its berries are ripe. The "berry" is a fleshy enlargement of the receptacle. The tiny "seeds" are the real fruit, know as achenes. Wild strawberry reproduces by runners from its stems as well as from seed.

Wild strawberry is often confused with cinquefoil (*Potentilla spp.*) because of the similar flowers and habitat. An examination of the leaves will prove definitive. Cinquefoil leaves are divided into five leaflets (as the name "cinque" implies), while strawberry leaves have only three leaflets. Wild strawberry leaves are edible if brewed into a tea and are said to be a good source of vitamin C.

♦ **HABITAT**—Dry fields and slopes.
♦ **LOCATIONS**—Rich Mountain Road, Bradley Fork Trail.
♦ **BLOOMS  APRIL - JUNE**

# PENNYWORT

*Obolaria virginica*

Gentian Family
(*Gentianaceae*)

Plant: 3″-6″
(8-15 cm)
Flower: ¼″-½″ long
(0.7-1.5cm)

Low elevation
Occasional

Jessie M. Harris

Inconspicuous is the word to keep in mind when looking for penny-wort. It is a diminutive plant—usually only 3″ (76 mm) tall. But once you've found one plant, stop to look for more nearby. The purplish-green color of the fleshy stem and sessile opposite leaves make penny-wort inconspicuous against the fallen leaves on the forest floor. The flowers are pale white or lavender, and even when fully open in early spring, are easily overlooked. Most botanists agree that pennywort is a hemi-saprophyte, able to do some photosynthesis with its own chlor-phyll. However, it probably derives most of its nutrition from fungus harbored in its roots (mycorrhizae) that take up nutrients from decay-ing matter in the leaf litter (humus).

◆ **HABITAT:** Moist, nutrient-rich woods.
◆ **LOCATION:** Turkey Pen Ridge Trail.
◆ **BLOOMS MARCH - APRIL**

Buttercup Family
(*Ranunculaceae*)

Plant: 6"-24"
(1.5-6 dm)
Flower: ⅛"-½"
(5-10 mm)

Wide range
Frequent

Jessie M. Harris

Brook meadowrue is a southern Appalachian endemic; that is, it is native to a restricted geographic area. The Smoky Mountains are within its range (Virginia to northern Georgia), and have ample habitat, so this relatively rare wildflower is found frequently in the park. Note how the flowers lack petals, but have showy white sepals. Unlike many other species of *Thalictrum* found in the park, brook meadowrue has perfect flowers, both male (pollen-producing) and female (seed-producing) organs in each flower. Each flower has numerous pollen-producing stamens that are readily visible with a hand lens. The seeds of brook meadowrue are shaped like a crescent moon. The open, long-stalked, and lacey appearance of the clusters of flowers and foliage give this plant its alternate common name, lady rue.

◆ **HABITAT**—Rich moist woods, seepage slopes, brook banks, waterfalls.
◆ **BLOOMS MAY - JULY**

# FRINGED PHACELIA

*Phacelia fimbriata*

Waterleaf family
(*Hydrophyllaceae*)

Plant: 6"
(15 cm)
Flower: ½"
(1.3 cm)

Mid-high elevation
Common

Adam Jones

These early spring ephemerals, with their white, deeply fringed flowers, are so densely packed it can look as if a light snow has recently fallen. The five petals are arranged to produce a cup-shaped flower that fades to purple as it ages. The alternate leaves are about 2" long with several triangular lobes. Although there are three other species of phacelia found in the park, none exhibit *P. fimbriata's* deep fringes.

In a landscape dominated by perennials and long-lived trees, this is one notable exception—a winter annual! The whole plant disappears quickly after flowering, leaving only its tiny brown seeds to resow the area. An amazing display of fringed phacelia can be seen at Chimneys Picnic Area during the first two weeks of April.

◆ **HABITAT**—Moist woods.
◆ **LOCATIONS**—Newfound Gap Road, Chimney Tops Trail.
◆ **BLOOMS MARCH - MAY**

*Silene stellata*

# STARRY CAMPION

Pink Family
(*Caryophyllaceae*)

Plant: 12″-36″
(30-92 cm)
Flower: ¾″
(1.9 cm)

Low-mid elevation
Frequent

Jessie M. Harris

A casual glimpse of this flower could fool you. What appears to be numerous petals are in fact only five deeply-notched ones forming a lacey star. This trait gives us the common name for its family, the pinks (as in "pinking" shears). The leaves are mostly whorled (in fours) along the tall stem. The five other members of the genus *Silene* found in the Smokies have just two leaves per node.

The base of the flower is balloon or bladder-like. You may find butterflies, bees, and moths visiting it. This is the most common summer campion in the park.

*Silene* is derived from the Greek for saliva. It refers to the sap of the stem.

◆ **HABITATS**—Open woods with rich soils.
◆ **LOCATIONS**—Balsam Mountain Road, Noland Divide Trail.
◆ **BLOOMS JULY - SEPTEMBER**

# WHITE TRILLIUM    *Trillium grandiflorum*

Lily Family
(*Liliaceae*)

Plant: 8"-18"
(20-46 cm)
Flower: 2"-4"
(5-10 cm)

Low-mid elevation
Common

Bill Lea

One of the showiest of the trilliums, white trillium's huge single flower stands on a stalk above the whorl of the three leaves character-istic of the trilliums. The flower's three large petals with wavy edges are usually white but turn various shades of pink as the flower fades with age. This color change signals to insects and other pollinators that pollination has already occurred.

Native Americans chewed the rhizomes of this species to ward off the effects of snakebite. In 1934, a botanist celebrated the dedication of the national park by writing that the trilliums were at last safe from feral pigs. Little did he know that by 1950 European wild hogs would permanently establish themselves in the Smokies.

◆ **HABITAT**—Moist woods, coves.
◆ **LOCATIONS**—Newfound Gap Road, Cove Hardwood Nature Tr.
◆ **BLOOMS APRIL - MAY**

*Trillium catesbaei*

# CATESBY'S TRILLIUM

Lily family
(*Liliaceae*)

Plant: 8"-20"
(20-51 cm)
Flower: 2"-3"
(5-8 cm)

Low-mid elevation
Frequent

Ed Ponikwia

Atop a green to purple stem sits the characteristic whorl of three elliptic leaves which makes trilliums easy to identify. The solitary nodding flower of Catesby's trillium varies from white to pale pink to deep rose. Because the petals of the more common white trillium (*T. grandiflorum*) may turn pink as they age, these two species can be confused. To tell the difference, note that the flower of the white trillium stands erect, while that of the Catesby's trillium hangs down.

Native to the southern Appalachians and the Piedmont of the Carolinas, this species was named for Mark Catesby, a 17th century English naturalist who explored the southeastern United States. Like some other spring wildflowers, trilliums have ant-dispersed seeds.

◆ **HABITAT**—Moist woods, mostly on the west side of the park.

◆ **LOCATIONS**—Rich Mountain Road, Cooper Road Trail.

◆ **BLOOMS MARCH - MAY**

# SWEET WHITE TRILLIUM

*Trillium simile*

Lily Family
(*Liliaceae*)

Plant: 8"-20"
(20-51 cm)
Flower: 2½"
(6 cm)

Mid elevation
Occasional

Tom Barnes

Sweet white trillium is so similar to wake robin (*T. erectum*) that it has been considered by some to be merely a variety of the latter. However, sweet white trillium is distinctive for its white flower (with a purple "eye") and pleasant smell. The whorl of three diamond-shaped leaves are positioned at the apex of the erect stem. The three petals which wreath the purple pistil in the center are spread out to make the flower appear rather flat in side view. The petals are broader than those of the similar looking white form of wake robin.

This attractive wildflower is found throughout the southern Appalachians, but it is nowhere as abundant as in the Smokies.

◆ **HABITAT**—Rich hardwood slopes, especially on the Tennessee side of the park.

◆ **LOCATIONS**—Little River Road, Chestnut Top Trail.

◆ **BLOOMS APRIL - MAY**

Lily Family
(*Liliaceae*)

Plant: 8"-20"
(20-51 cm)
Flower: 2"-2½"
(5-6 cm)

Wide range
Frequent

Harry Ellis

Rivaling the white trillium (*T. grandiflorum*) with its attractive-ness, painted trillium is easy to identify by the maroon "paint" nature has splashed on the inner base of each petal. The otherwise white petals display wavy margins and curve up and outwards to reveal the color-stained center, where the pink-tipped stamens reside. Three green sepals lie behind the petals. A shiny red berry develops from the ovary of the flower by August. Many trillium seeds are dispersed by ants.

Painted trillium reaches the southern-most extent of its range in the southern Appalachians. It is a plant of cool woods, following spruce and fir trees all the way to Canada.

◆ **HABITAT**—Dry to moist woods, trailsides.
◆ **LOCATIONS**—Balsam Mountain Road, The Boulevard Trail.
◆ **BLOOMS APRIL - MAY**

# WILD STONECROP

*Sedum ternatum*

Sedum Family:
(*Crassulaceae*)

Plant: 4"-5"
(10-13 cm)
Flower: ½"
(1.3 cm)

Low-mid elevation
Common

Ed Ponikwia

Narrow white petals and black-tipped anthers characterize this plant's flowers, but it's the three-spoked arrangement of the flowering stems that catch your attention. A careful examination of the plant will prove interesting. It has separate fertile and sterile shoots. The sterile shoots, with their succulent leaves in whorls of three, sit close to their rocky host. The fertile shoots have a basal whorl of leaves; additional leaves alternate on the stem.

Several non-native stonecrops can be found in the park. Mountain folklore claims they act as barometers. If sedum thrives near the home, good times will follow. Conversely, a withering plant foreshadows death.

◆ **HABITAT**—Moist, rocky slopes; on boulders and tree bases.

◆ **LOCATIONS**—Little River Road, Chestnut Top Trail.

◆ **BLOOMS  APRIL - JUNE**

# BOWMAN'S ROOT

Rose Family:
*(Rosaceae)*

Plant: 2'-4'
(0.6-1.2 m)
Flower: 1½"
(3.8 cm)

Low-mid elevation
Frequent

Harry Ellis

The alternate leaves of the bowman's root are divided into three distinct parts, hence the Latin name *trifoliatus*. The three serrated leaflets are long and narrow. Two sharply pointed "mini leaves" called stipules mark the base of the leaves.

The flower's five twisted white petals are of uneven length, lending the plant a somewhat tattered appearance. The petals radiate from a central tube covered by a pinkish calyx. Inside are 20 stamens and five pistils. These flowers are loosely grouped into a many-branched inflorescence called a panicle.

Common names include Indian-physic and American ipecac, because the crushed root induced vomiting.

◆ **HABITAT**—Dry woods.
◆ **LOCATIONS**—Rich Mountain Road, Noland Divide Trail.
◆ **BLOOMS APRIL - JUNE**

# WHORLED WOOD ASTER

*Aster acuminatus*

Aster Family
(*Asteraceae*)

Plant: 8″-15″
(20-37 cm)
Flower head: 1″-
1½″ (2.5-3.8 cm)

Mid-high elevation
Common

Jessie M. Harris

*leaf*

This aster has 10-17 white or pinkish rays (outer petals) surrounding yellow or red disk flowers. Bracts surrounding each head are sharply pointed, layered, and straw-colored (sometimes greenish or purplish). There are usually 10-22 leaves below the flower cluster, and the leaves crowd toward the top of the stem. Lower leaves are small and may be absent at flowering. Upper leaves have a few sharp teeth. Whorled wood aster has underground runners so it often forms large colonies.

There are more than 20 species of aster in the park, and they can be challenging to identify. Look at the entire plant—leaves, stem, flowers—to aid in identification. Habitat (wet or dry, sunny or shady) and elevation can also be important.

◆ **HABITAT**—Cool woods and slopes.

◆ **LOCATIONS**—Balsam Mountain Road, The Boulevard Trail.

◆ **BLOOMS JULY - SEPTEMBER**

# WHITE WOOD ASTER

Aster Family
(*Asteraceae*)

Plant: 12"-36"
(30-92 cm)
Flower head:
¾"-1"
(1.9-2.5 cm)

Low-mid elevation
Common

*ray flower*

Jessie M. Harris

This aster has daisy-like heads comprised of 5-10 white ray flowers and yellow or red central disk flowers. The leaves are thin in texture and are arranged alternately on the stem. The lower leaves are the largest (2"-6" long, 1"-3" wide), conspicuously pointed at the tip, heart-shaped at the base, and coarsely toothed. Leaves farther up the stem are progressively smaller, less stalked, and less heart-shaped. Similar big-leaved aster (*A. macrophyllus*) has thick basal leaves 3" or more wide, and lavender-violet (rarely white) rays. Mountain wood aster (*A. chlorolepsis*) has 10 or more ray flowers and grows only at high elevations.

Each aster flower head is actually a group of many tiny flowers.

◆ **HABITAT**—Woodlands.
◆ **LOCATIONS**—Clingmans Dome Road, Schoolhouse Gap Trail.
◆ **BLOOMS AUGUST - OCTOBER**

# SQUIRREL CORN

*Dicentra canadensis*

Fumitory Family
(*Fumariaceae*)

Plant: 5"-10"
(13-25 cm)
Flower: 1/2"
(1.3 cm)

Wide range
Frequent

Bill Lea

This fleeting spring perennial is easily confused with a close relative, Dutchman's britches (*D. cucullaria*). Both exhibit dissected compound leaves and have nodding white flowers that bloom about the same time. To make things more confusing, they are often found in the same habitats. However, the basic shapes of the flowers are different enough for the careful observer to quickly distinguish the two. The common name may come from the plant's small, yellow tubers which squirrels reportedly eat. Squirrel corn has a scent reminiscent of hyacinths.

Squirrel corn is apparently poisonous to cattle that ingest the tubers in the spring.

◆ **HABITAT**—Rich woods.
◆ **LOCATIONS**—Little River Road, Cove Hardwood Nature Trail.
◆ **BLOOMS APRIL - MAY**

*Dicentra cucullaria*

# DUTCHMAN'S BRITCHES

Fumitory Family
(*Fumariaceae*)

Plant: 5"-10"
(13-25 cm)
Flower: ¾"
(1.9 cm)

Wide range
Common

Mary Ann Kressig

It's not difficult to imagine how this spring ephemeral got its name—the shape of the white flower reminds one of a pair of pantaloons hung out on the line to dry. The leafless flowering stalk arches over the bluish, finely dissected leaves, which stand upright. The roots of this delicate, short-lived species possess creamy white bulblets.

"Dicentra" is Greek for two spurs, referring to the flower's two "legs." Early bumblebees have a long proboscis, which allows them to tap the nectar contained deep within these flowers. Native Americans throughout eastern North America dried the bulbs for use as a spring tonic and blood purifier.

◆ **HABITAT**—Rich woods.
◆ **LOCATIONS**—Balsam Mountain Road, Cove Hardwood Nature Trail.
◆ **BLOOMS APRIL - MAY**

# FALSE BUGBANE

*Trautvetteria caroliniensis*

Buttercup Family
(*Ranunculaceae*)

Plant: 18"-5'
(0.5 - 1.5 m)
Flower: ½"-¾"
(1-2 cm)

Wide range
Occasional

Jessie M. Harris

False bugbane is a robust perennial wildflower that likes the damp soil along streams and cool hardwood forests. While the leaves at the base of the plant have long stalks, the upper leaves may be sessile or only short stalked. Each dark green glossy leaf has 5-11 lobes, and each lobe may itself be dissected, lobed, or serrate to some degree.

The flowers, while showy, have no petals! Instead, the numerous feathery white stamens, the pollen-producing organs of the flower, are the main attraction. Each stamen can be up to half an inch long (1 cm)! False bugbane is a wind-pollinated plant, but you may see insects visiting the plant to eat protein-rich pollen. There is but a single species of *Trautvetteria* in North America.

- ◆ **HABITAT:** Damp forests and streambanks.
- ◆ **LOCATION:** Road Prong Trail.
- ◆ **BLOOMS LATE MAY - JULY**

*Laportea canadensis*

Nettle Family
(*Urticaceae*)

Plant: 2'-4'
(0.6-1.2 m)
Flower: spikes of
exceedingly small
flowers

Wide range
Common

Harry Ellis

Y ou may not want to examine this wildflower too closely; the "hairs" on the stem and leaves sting! The leaves are coarsely toothed and arranged alternately on the stem. Spikes of male flowers (those producing pollen) are found in the joints of the lower leaves. Female flowers (those producing seeds) are found in spreading spikes from the upper leaf joints and from the top of the plant. False nettle (*Boehmeria cylindrica*) and richweed (*Pilea pumila*) resemble wood-nettle, but both lack stinging hairs.

Formic acid and bicarbonate of ammonia are what give this plant its sting. Juice of dock plants (*Rumex*) is said to relieve the nettle's sting: "Nettle in, dock out. Dock rub nettle out."

◆ **HABITAT**—Rich woods, stream banks, and disturbed sites.
◆ **LOCATIONS**—Newfound Gap Road, Bote Mountain Trail.
◆ **BLOOMS JUNE - AUGUST**

# INDIAN PIPE

*Monotropa uniflora*

Indian Pipe
Family
(*Monotropaceae*)

Plant: 3"-8"
(8-20 cm)
Flower: ½"-1"
(1.3-2.5 cm)

Wide range
Common

Ken Voorhis

*upright seed
capsule*

Although you may mistake it for a fungus, Indian pipe is in fact a flowering plant. It lacks the green pigment chlorophyll and so can not make its own food. Consequently, it lives as a saprophyte, garnering nourishment from decaying organic matter in the soil.

Upon fertilization, the flower will turn upright, which may explain the genus name *Monotropa* (one-turn). Pine-sap (*M. hypopithys*) is a similar plant but has several pink or tawny flowers per stem.

Cherokee legend claims that long ago the Cherokee god caught the seven clans' leaders smoking the peace pipe before an argument had been settled. Infuriated, he destroyed the council. As a reminder, Indian pipe now grows in places where kin once argued.

◆ **HABITAT**—Woodlands.
◆ **LOCATIONS**—Rich Mountain Road, Cooper Road Trail.
◆ **BLOOMS JUNE - SEPTEMBER**

## *Tiarella cordifolia*

# FOAMFLOWER

Saxifrage Family
(*Saxifragaceae*)

Plant: 6"-12"
(15-30 cm)
Flower: numer-
ous small flowers
in a spike 1"-6"
long, 1" wide

Wide range
Common

Bill Lea

This spring wildflower is easily recognized by its delicate spike of white flowers on a hairy, leafless stalk. Each leaf is shallowly lobed, toothed, and resembles a maple leaf. The leaves rise from the base of the plant on long, hairy stems. The flower's ten stamens are conspicuous. Foamflower is similar to alumroot (*Heuchera americana*), a taller plant, and to bishop's cap (*Mitella diphylla*), a wildflower with two leaves on the flowering stalk.

The scientific name for foamflower describes its flower and leaf characters. "Tiarella" means "little crown" and refers to the shape of the seed-producing organ, and "cordifolia" refers to the heart-shaped base of each leaf.

◆ **HABITAT**—Moist woodlands and stream banks.
◆ **LOCATIONS**—Little River Road, Bradley Fork Trail.
◆ **BLOOMS  APRIL - JUNE**

# BISHOP'S CAP

*Mitella diphylla*

Saxifrage Family
(*Saxifragaceae*)

Plant: 6"-18"
(15-46 cm)
Flower: under ½"
(1.3 cm)

Low-mid elevation
Frequent

Ed Ponikwia

*flower petal*

Bishop's cap has a single pair of opposite leaves half-way up the flowering stalk. The leaves at the base of the plant are long-stalked, hairy, and resemble maple leaves. Five to twenty minute flowers form a spike that is 4"-8" long. Take a close look at an individual flower with a hand lens—the five fringed petals resemble a snowflake. Bishop's cap is related to foamflower (*Tiarella cordifolia*), which lacks leaves on the flowering stalk, and alumroot (*Heuchera americana*), which has greenish-purple flowers.

"Mitella" is Latin for cap. This refers to the shape of the seed. "Diphylla" means "two leaves" and refers to the prominent pair of leaves on the flowering stem.

♦ **HABITAT**—Rich woods.
♦ **LOCATIONS**—Rich Mountain Road, Chestnut Top Trail.
♦ **BLOOMS APRIL - MAY**

# DOWNY RATTLESNAKE-PLANTAIN

*Goodyera pubescens*

Orchid Family
(*Orchidaceae*)

Plant: Flowering
stalk 8″-16″
(20-41 cm)

Low-mid elevation
Common

*dried fruits*

Jessie M. Harris

Downy rattlesnake-plantain is one of the most easily recognized wild-flowers year-round due to its distinctive evergreen leaves. The egg-shaped leaves are found at the base of the plant in a rosette. They are bluish-green with prominent white veins which give the leaf a "snake skin" look. The dried fruits are round and clustered like the rattle of a rattlesnake. Lesser rattlesnake-plantain (G. *repens*) is a smaller, less common plant found mostly on the east side of the park.

Downy rattlesnake-plantain can be found throughout eastern North America and is one of the most common orchids in the park. Its common name refers to its veiny leaves and fruit cluster, not to any use for snake bites.

- ◆ **HABITAT**—Woodlands.
- ◆ **LOCATIONS**—Balsam Mountain Road, Porters Creek Trail.
- ◆ **BLOOMS JUNE - AUGUST**

# GALAX

*Galax urceolata*

Diapensia Family
(*Diapensiaceae*)

Plant: 12"-24"
(30-61 cm)
Flower: ⅙"
(0.4 cm)

Wide range
Common

Jessie M. Harris

Whatever the season, galax will reward you with its beauty. In the early spring, its round, evergreen leaves carpet the dormant forest floor. By summer, a tall pillar of tiny white flowers lines many park trails. Then, as winter approaches, the deep green leaves turn bronze and crimson to contrast against the coming snows.

Galax comes from the Greek *gala*, meaning milky. This refers to the five milky-white petals of the tiny flowers. Their garlic-like odor attracts flies and other insect pollinators. Galax grows vigorously after forest fires.

Galax occurs only in the southern Appalachians and was once in peril because of over-collection for floral arrangements.

◆ **HABITAT**—Dry woods.
◆ **LOCATIONS**—Rich Mountain Road, Cooper Road Trail.
◆ **BLOOMS MAY - JUNE**

## *Amianthium muscitoxicum*

# FLY POISON

Bunchflower Family
(*Melanthiaceae*)

Plant: 1'-4'
(0.3-1.2 m)
Flower: ¼"-½"
(0.6-1.3 cm)

High elevation
Occasional

Jay Kranyik

A dense, cylindrical cluster of creamy white flowers towers above the grass-like basal leaves of this perennial. After pollination, the flowers persist, turning green to greenish-purple with age. The fruit is a three-beaked, dark brown capsule containing many red-coated seeds.

The alkaloids present in all parts of fly poison are toxic enough to kill livestock and presumably humans as well. Parts of the plant were once used to attract and exterminate flies. One folk recipe calls for the crushed bulb to be mixed with sugar and placed strategically around the house and barn. The species name comes from the Latin for fly (muscae) and poison (toxicum). It is the only species in the genus *Amianthium*.

◆ **HABITAT**—Moist woods, especially oak forests.
◆ **LOCATIONS**—Balsam Mountain Road, Noland Divide Trail.
◆ **BLOOMS MAY - JUNE**

# Fairy Wand

*Chamaelirium luteum*

Bunchflower Family
*(Melanthiaceae)*

Plant: 1'-4'
(0.3-1.2 m)
Flower: ⅛"-¼"
(0.3-0.6 cm)

Low-mid elevation
Frequent

Jessie M. Harris

*female flower*

The delightful common name for this plant comes from the appearance of the infloresence, a dense, elongated cluster of little white flowers from 4"-8" long on a wand-like stalk. This species is *dioecious*, literally "two houses" in Greek, meaning the male and female flowers reside on separate plants. On the male plant (photo above) the wand is tapered and gracefully arches, while the female plant displays a shorter, slenderer, upright version. The females are generally less numerous in a population of fairy wands. The leaves at the base of the plant are spoon-shaped and are broadest near the tips.

The specific name *luteum* comes from the color of the male flowers which have a yellowish cast due to the yellow stamens.

◆ **HABITAT**—Woods and thickets.
◆ **LOCATIONS**—Laurel Creek Road, Schoolhouse Gap Trail.
◆ **BLOOMS APRIL - MAY**

*Spiranthes cernua*

Orchid Family
*(Orchidaceae)*

Plant: 4"-18"
(10-45 cm)
Flower: Small
flowers in 1"-7"
spike (2.5-18 cm)

Wide range
Frequent

Harry Ellis

The largest leaves (2"-10" long, less than 1" wide) of this orchid are at the base of the plant. The leaves reduce in size up the stem until they are merely scales at the top. The flowers are packed into a dense spiraling spike. The flowers are small, white, horizontal to the ground or slightly nodding, and usually fragrant.

The name for the genus comes from Greek "*speira,*" meaning coil, and refers to the twisted spike of flowers. There are six species of lady's tresses in the park, with nodding lady's tresses being the most common. The species differ in the tightness of the spiral of flowers, habitat, and blooming season. Another common name for this plant is autumn tresses, which refers to its season of bloom.

- ◆ **HABITAT**—Wet woods, meadows, and stream margins.
- ◆ **LOCATIONS**—Cades Cove Loop Road, Forney Ridge Trail.
- ◆ **BLOOMS AUGUST - FROST**

# MOUNTAIN BUGBANE    *Cimicifuga americana*

Buttercup Family
(*Ranunculaceae*)

Plant: 3'-5'
(0.9-1.5 m)
Flower: ¼"
(0.6 cm)

Mid elevation
Common

Harry Ellis

This large plant can be identified by its alternate, coarsely toothed, compound leaves and its tall (up to 1') clusters of tiny flowers. Take a close look at these unusual flowers. Without petals and with short-lived sepals, it is the stamens which provide the splash of white. These cleft or two-horned structures attract pollinating insects to the 3-8 stalked carpels at the center of the blossom.

The very similar black cohosh (*C. racemosa*) can be differentiated by one-horned stamens and a single (rarely two) stalkless carpel. Better yet, just smell each plant. Black cohosh has a very strong odor. It is pollinated by carrion beetles attracted to the offensive scent.

*Cimicifuga* means to drive away bugs.

◆ **HABITAT**—Rich woods.
◆ **LOCATIONS**—Rich Mountain Road, Gregory Ridge Trail.
◆ **BLOOMS JULY ‑ SEPTEMBER**

Bunchflower Family
(*Melanthiaceae*)

Plant: 1'-5'
(0.3 to 1.5 m)
Flower: ⅛"-¼"
(4-10 mm)

Wide range
Occasional

Jessie M. Harris

Featherbells may not have big flowers, but it certainly has copious quantities of small ones! Each individual flower is minute, but the cluster of flowers (the inflorescence) can be more than a foot (3 dm) long. Each flower has 6 white petals, and 6 stamens around the female, seed-producing capsule. The flowers are insect-pollinated and perhaps wind-pollinated as well. The leaves are strongly ribbed and linear (8-28" [2-7 dm] long; and only about ¾" [17 mm] wide), though they reduce rapidly in length toward the inflorescence. The species name, *gramineum*, means *grass-like*. While featherbells has traditionally been placed in the Lily family, many botanists now place it in the Bunchflower family based upon molecular (DNA) evidence.

♦ **HABITAT**—Thin woodlands, meadows, dry upland forests.

♦ **BLOOMS JULY - SEPTEMBER**

# ONE-FLOWERED CANCER-ROOT

Jessie M. Harris

*Orobanche uniflora*

Broom-rape Family
(*Orobanchaceae*)

Plant: 3"-5"
(8 to 14 cm)
Flower: 1"
(2.5 cm)

Low-mid elevation
Scarce

One-flowered cancer-root is a subtle wildflower. Even when there are many plants in full bloom, it is easily overlooked. The plant is only 3"-5" tall, and each fleshy, straw-colored stem bears a solitary, inch-long, pale lavender flower. The blossom, stem, and scale-like leaves are covered with glandular hairs. As is typical of all other members of the Broom-rape family, one-flowered cancer-root lacks chlorophyll (green pigment) and is parasitic on a wide variety of plants (oaks, asters, and *Sedum* to name just a few). "Orobos" means "to strangle" in Greek, and our common name, cancer-root, alludes to its parasitic nature. Cancer-root is an annual, pollinated by insects, and each flower produces 500-5,000 minute seeds that are dispersed by wind and water.

♦ **HABITAT**—Riverbanks, road edges.
♦ **LOCATIONS**—Little River, Albright Grove Loop trails.
♦ **BLOOMS  APRIL - MAY**

# FALSE SOLOMON'S SEAL

*Maianthemum racemosum*

Lily Family
(*Liliaceae*)

Plant: 12"-36"
(30-90 cm)
Flower: -⅛"
(0.3 cm)

Wide range
Common

Joseph G. Strauch, Jr.

Tiny starbursts of creamy white flowers form a large pyramidal cluster atop this late-spring to summer blooming perennial. A ruby-red, translucent berry takes the place of each fertilized flower. Quite similar in appearance to the true Solomon's seals (*Polygonatum spp.*), they are easily differentiated by the position of the flowers and fruits. Here they are clustered at the end of the plant, while the true Solomon's seals display two or three flowers beneath each leaf along the length of the stem. Some people remember the difference with the rhyme, "Solomon's seal, to be real, must have flowers along its keel." This species also lacks the seal-like pattern seen in the rhizomes of the true Solomon's seals.

♦ **HABITAT**—Moist woods.
♦ **LOCATIONS**—Tremont Road, Cove Hardwood Nature Trail.
♦ **BLOOMS MAY - JUNE**

# SMOOTH SOLOMON'S SEAL

Jessie M. Harris

*Polygonatum biflorum var. biflorum*

Lily Family
(*Liliaceae*)

Plant: 1'-4'
(0.3-1.2 m)
Flower: ½"-¾"
(1.3-1.9 cm)

Low-mid elevation
Common

The small, tubular flowers of the Solomon's seal hang hidden below the leaves on the gracefully arching stems. The leaves are hairless. As the name suggests, a similar species, hairy Solomon's seal (*P. pubescens*) is distinguished by the minute hairs that trace each vein on the underside of the leaves. Another subspecies, *P. biflorum* var. *commutatum*, is a larger version of smooth Solomon's seal.

Smooth Solomon's seal can be easily distinguished from the false Solomon's seal (*Maianthemum racemosum*) by the location of the flowers; they are hidden beneath the leaves on the smooth, while the flowers of the false are clustered at the end of the stem. The round scars on the roots of this plant are said to resemble a wax "seal."

◆ **HABITAT**—Moist woods.
◆ **LOCATIONS**—Roaring Fork Motor Nature Tr., Porters Creek Tr.
◆ **BLOOMS APRIL - MAY**

## *Saxifraga micranthidifolia*

# BROOK LETTUCE

Saxifrage Family
(*Saxifragaceae*)

Plant: flowering
stalk 12″-30″
(30-76 cm)
Flower: ½″ flowers
in large, broad clus-
ter (1.3 cm)

Low-mid elevation
Common

Harry Ellis

One important key to identifying this plant is its habitat: it is found in shady mountain brooks and wet seepage slopes. Its large leaves (up to 12″ long, 3″ wide) are hard to miss. Each leaf has 12-40 coarse teeth per side. The flowering stalk is branched above the middle and topped by a large, open cluster of tiny flowers. Each flower is radially symmetrical, and each petal is white with a yellow spot at the base. Michaux's saxifrage (*S. michauxii*) looks similar, but it grows only at the park's high elevations and its flowers are bilaterally symmetrical.

This plant is a southern and central Appalachian endemic. That is, it is found nowhere else in the world besides the region from eastern Pennsylvania south to southwestern South Carolina.

◆ **HABITAT**—Streams and seepage slopes.
◆ **LOCATIONS**—Balsam Mountain Road, Kanati Fork Trail.
◆ **BLOOMS MAY - JUNE**

# Michaux's Saxifrage

Harry Ellis

*Saxifraga michauxii*

Saxifrage Family
(*Saxifragaceae*)

Plant: flowering
stalk 4"-16"
(10-41 cm)
Flower: ¼"
(0.6 cm)

High elevation
Common

Although this wildflower could be mistaken for brook lettuce (*S. micranthidifolia*), take a closer look and you will find many differences. While both plants may grow on seepage slopes, Michaux's saxifrage will tolerate drier and sunnier sites. It is the only saxifrage in the park with bilaterally symmetrical flowers. Also, Michaux's grows only at high elevation, while brook lettuce is seldom found above 4,500'.

Michaux's saxifrage lives only in the southern Appalachians. It is one of the first plants to colonize high elevation landslide scars in the park. The species name "michauxii" honors the plant's discoverer, Andre Michaux (1746-1802). Michaux, botanist for King Louis XVI of France, collected many plants in North America.

◆ **HABITAT**—Seepage slopes and exposed rock outcrops.
◆ **LOCATIONS**—Newfound Gap Road, Noland Divide Trail.
◆ **BLOOMS JUNE - AUGUST**

## *Diphylleia cymosa*

# UMBRELLA LEAF

Barberry Family
(*Berberidaceae*)

Plant: 1′-3′
(30-90 cm)
Flower: 0.5″-1″
(1.3-2.5 cm)

Mid-high elevation
Frequent

Bill Lea

Like its close relative, may-apple (*Podophyllum peltatum*), the leaves of this plant look like an open umbrella left standing in the woods. However, its small cluster of white, six-petaled flowers rises on a stalk above the broad, coarsely-toothed leaves. The flowering stalk has two leaves. All the leaves are peltate, meaning the leaf attachment is near the center of the leaf, not at an edge. This species is perhaps most interesting later in summer when the deep blue berries contrast sharply with the bright red fruiting stalks.

   Although not listed as poisonous, umbrella leaf seems to have had few medicinal or edible uses. It is found only in the southern Appalachians.

◆ **HABITAT**—Streamsides and seepage areas.
◆ **LOCATIONS**—Newfound Gap Road, Little River Trail.
◆ **BLOOMS APRIL - JUNE**

# LARGER ENCHANTER'S-NIGHTSHADE

Jessie M. Harris

*Circaea lutetiana*
ssp. *canadensis*

Evening Primrose
Family
(*Onagraceae*)

Plant: 1'-2'
(30-60 cm)
Flower: up to ⅛"
(0.3 cm)

Low-mid elevation
Frequent

This wildflower is more notable when in fruit than in flower. The fruits are small burrs that persist well into winter. The plant is usually knee-high, with one or several branching spikes of white flowers at the top of the stem. The leaves are opposite, toothed, and on long stalks. Smaller enchanter's-nightshade (*C. alpina*) is a much smaller plant, never more than 6" tall. It is frequent in seepage areas at high elevations in the park.

Plants use a variety of methods to disperse their seeds, (*e.g.* wind, water, and animals). Larger and smaller enchanter's-nightshade depend on animals walking by and accidentally picking up burred seeds.

◆ **HABITAT**—Rich woods.
◆ **LOCATIONS**—Cades Cove Loop Road, Schoolhouse Gap Trail.
◆ **BLOOMS JUNE - AUGUST**

*Convallaria
majuscula*

Lily family
*(Liliaceae)*

Plant: 6"-12"
(15-35 cm)
Flower: ¼"
(7 mm)

Mid elevation
Scarce

Jessie M. Harris

Don't mistake this native wildflower for its cultivated, European cousin *(Convallaria majalis)*. Both have delicate coral white flowers that nod on a slender stalk. However, note that the native's flowering stalk is less than half as long as the leaves (the cultivated species has longer stalks). Second, individuals of the native species are widely scattered, not colonial (plants no more than 2"-4" apart) as the European species is. Lastly, the European species is found only around homesites. Wild lily-of-the-valley is a southern Appalachian endemic. Prevent children and pets from eating either species of lily-of-the-valley—toxins found throughout the plant cause abdominal pain, diarrhea, and slow pulse.

◆ **HABITAT**—Montane oak forests, ridgetops.
◆ **LOCATION**—Cataloochee Divide Trail.
◆ **BLOOMS APRIL - JUNE**

# DWARF GINSENG

*Panax trifolius*

Ginseng Family
(*Araliaceae*)

Plant: 2"-8"
(.5-2 dm)
Inflorescence Size:
1/2"-1" diameter
(12-25 mm)

Mid elevation
Scarce

Ken Voorhis

Ginseng is relatively easy to find in the park—you just have to be looking for the *right* ginseng! Dwarf ginseng is not valuable commercially or medicinally, and so it is more plentiful than its prized cousin, Sang (*Panax quinquefolius*). Dwarf ginseng is a minute plant, so you will have to look carefully. The single stem arises from a round root deep in the soil. The stem branches into 3 leaves (each leaf has 3-5 elliptic, serrate leaflets) and a single flowering stem terminating in an umbel. Yellowish-green berries ripen August-October. There are a dozen species in the genus *Panax*: 10 in east Asia and 2 in North America. *Panacea* and *Panax* are both from Greek, *pas* (all) and *akos* (cure), literally, a cure-all.

◆ **HABITAT**—Rich woods, damp clearings, cove forests.

◆ **LOCATION**—Porters Creek Trail.

◆ **BLOOMS APRIL - JUNE**

## *Clintonia umbellulata*          SPECKLED WOOD LILY

Lily Family
(*Liliaceae*)

Plant: 8"-20"
(20-51 cm)
Flower: ½"
(1.3 cm)

Mid elevation
Frequent

*berries*

Jessie M. Harris

The flowers of this plant have six identical sepals and petals that are white with purple and green speckles. Displayed in a cluster, they bloom but briefly and are quickly replaced by an upright clump of round, shiny, (and poisonous) black berries that ripen later in the summer. Another species of *Clintonia* also inhabits the park. Commonly called bluebead lily (*C. borealis*), it has fewer and yellow flowers that tend to nod and berries that are bright blue and oval. Bluebead lily is found only at high elevation in the park.

The genus *Clintonia* was named for New York governor and naturalist DeWitt Clinton (1769-1828). Henry David Thoreau complained that this beautiful group of plants was named for a politician.

◆ **HABITAT**—Moist woods.

◆ **LOCATIONS**—Roaring Fork M.N.T., Noland Divide Trail.

◆ **BLOOMS MAY - JUNE**

107

# CANADA MAYFLOWER

Jessie M. Harris

*Maianthemum canadense*

Lily Family
*(Liliaceae)*

Plant: 2"-6"
(5-15 cm)
Flower: ¼"
(0.6 cm)

Mid-high elevation
Occasional

This plant is a rather unusual member of the Lily family in that the flower parts are in twos and fours instead of the usual threes and sixes. A small dense cluster of tiny white flowers, each having a starburst appearance, top this low growing perennial. The 1-3 leaves have an elongated heart shape and are shiny, smooth, and deep green. They often occur in dense beds.

In leaf, one could confuse Canada mayflower with a true lily-of-the-valley (*Convallaria*). This has led to an alternate common name, false lily-of-the-valley. However, the true lily-of-the-valley has bell-shaped flowers. Canada mayflower sports a cluster of red, translucent berries throughout the winter.

◆ **HABITAT**—Moist woods.

◆ **LOCATIONS**—Balsam Mountain Road, Noland Divide Trail.

◆ **BLOOMS MAY - JULY**

## *Aruncus dioicus*

Rose Family
(*Rosaceae*)

Plant: 3'-6'
(0.9-1.8 m)
Flower: up to ¼"
(0.6 cm)

Low-mid elevation
Frequent

*terminal leaflet*

Bill Lea

This robust plant can be easily mistaken for false goat's-beard (*Astilbe biternata*), a member of the Saxifrage family. Both plants have compound leaves with toothed leaflets. However, the terminal (end) leaflet of goat's-beard has no lobes while false goat's beard has three lobes. True goat's-beard flowers have 15 or more stamens; false goat's-beard flowers have 10 stamens.

Goat's beard is dioecious; having separate male and female plants. The male flower, with its five white petals and 15-20 white stamens, is the more showy. The female flower has three pistils at its center. Interestingly, it also has tiny, non-functional stamens as well, perhaps indicating a perfect (having both male and female parts) ancestry.

◆ **HABITAT**—Rich woods and seeps.
◆ **LOCATIONS**—Rich Mountain Road, Noland Divide Trail.
◆ **BLOOMS MAY - JULY**

# WHITE BANEBERRY

*Actaea pachypoda*

Buttercup Family
(*Ranunculaceae*)

Plant: 1′-2′
(30-60 cm)
Flower: ¼″
(0.6 cm)

Wide range
Frequent

Jessie M. Harris

*berries*

This common plant is more often noticed when in fruit than in flower. Numerous tiny white flowers rise above its compound leaves which are divided into three leaflets. Minute petals surround numerous yellow-tipped, club-shaped stamens and a single pistil. These inconspicuous blossoms are arranged in a cluster up to 8″ tall.

From July to October this plant is often called "doll's eyes," because of its large white berries. A dark central spot on these round berries remind many of the porcelain eyes of old-time dolls. The term "bane" was used to indicate that a plant is poisonous. As the name implies, it is the berries that are thought to be harmful.

◆ **HABITAT**— Rich woods.

◆ **LOCATIONS**—Roaring Fork Motor Nature Trail, Kanati Fork Trail.

◆ **BLOOMS APRIL - MAY**

*Pycnanthemum montanum*

# MOUNTAIN-MINT

Mint Family
(*Lamiaceae*)

Plant: 18″-30″
(46-76 cm)
Flower: numerous
tiny flowers in
round heads ¾″ in
diameter (1.9 cm)

Low-mid elevation
Frequent

*mint stem*

Jessie M. Harris

Mountain-mint has tiny flowers in dense heads at the ends of branches. Each individual flower is creamy with many purple spots. Use a magnifying glass to appreciate the delicate structure of the two-lipped blossoms. The largest leaves (3″ long, 1″ wide) are toward the base of the plant. All leaves are coarsely toothed and paired along the squarish stem. All parts of the plant are fragrant. Mountain-mint can be enjoyed year-round because its dried seed heads remain on the stalks well into winter.

The scientific name for this plant describes its appearance and habitat. "Pycnos" means "dense" in Greek, "anthemum" means "flower," and "montanum" means "of the mountains."

◆ **HABITAT**—Open woods.
◆ **LOCATIONS**—Balsam Mountain Road, Little River Trail.
◆ **BLOOMS JUNE - AUGUST**

# RAMPS

*Allium tricoccum*

Lily Family
(*Liliaceae*)

Plant: 6"-16"
(15-41 cm)
Flower: ⅓"
(0.8 cm)

Mid-high elevation
Frequent

Joseph G. Strauch, Jr.

Ramps are perhaps more distinctive for their spring leaves than their summer flowers. The 2-3 leaves (6"-10" long, up to 3" wide) appear in April and are gone by the time the plant flowers. The tiny, pale, yellow or cream, bell-shaped blossoms are grouped in a tight cluster about 1½" wide. Ramps are similar to the wild onions and are sometimes called wild leeks.

Traditionally ramps were dug for food during the Zodiac sign Aries. The symbol for Aries is the ram and this plant was called "ram's son." This was shortened over the years to "ramps." Although eating the oniony roots of this plant is still popular locally, research has shown that over-collecting can lead to marked declines in ramp populations. Digging ramps is now banned in the park.

◆ **HABITAT**—Rich, moist soils of sheltered coves.
◆ **BLOOMS JUNE - JULY**

*Asclepias exaltata*

# POKE MILKWEED

Milkweed Family
(*Asclepiadaceae*)

Plant: 1'-3'
(5-10 dm)
Flower: umbels 2"-4" broad
(5-10 cm)

Low to middle
Frequent

Jessie M. Harris

This showy wildflower is worthy of exaltation! Poke milkweed is a robust wildflower—up to 3 feet tall-with large opposite leaves—and a stout stem with milky juice. A single plant will have 2-4 showy inflorescences, groups of 20 or more flowers arranged in an umbel. Each individual flower is on a long stalk (pedicel, ½"-1¾"). Poke milkweed pods (½" - ¾" broad, 4½"-5 ½" long) mature in August or September and release hundreds of seeds. Each seed has a parachute of silky threads for wind dispersal. Monarch butterfly (*Danaus plexippus*) caterpillars feed exclusively on milkweeds in the genus *Asclepias*. Look for the vivid black, yellow, and white-striped larvae on poke milkweed leaves.

**HABITAT**—Moist forests, slopes and forest edges.
**LOCATION**—Cades Cove meadows.
**BLOOMS JUNE - JULY**

# FRASER'S SEDGE

*Cymophyllus fraseriana*

Sedge Family
(*Cyperaceae*)

Plant: 4"-15"
(10-38 cm)
Flower spike:
½"-1"
(1.3-2.5 cm)

Low-mid elevation
Occasional

Jessie M. Harris

This evergreen plant may at first be mistaken for a member of the Lily family. Closely examine the strap-like leaves, however, and you will notice the wavy leaf-margins with short stiff hairs and the absence of a mid-vein. In fact, the name *Cymophyllus* means "wavy leaf" in Greek. In some plants the leaves may measure up to 2'. The single flower spike bears female flowers below and male flowers above.

Once familiar with Fraser's sedge, you will understand just how unusual it is. It is found only in the southern and central Appalachians and is the only member of the genus *Cymophyllus* in the world. In the Smokies it is most common in forests that were never logged.

♦ **HABITAT**—Rich woods, often old-growth forests.
♦ **LOCATIONS**—Laurel Creek Road, Bradley Fork Trail.
♦ **BLOOMS APRIL - JUNE**

*Antennaria neglecta*

Aster Family
(*Asteraceae*)

Plant: 4"-16"
(10-41 cm)
Flower head: ¼"-½"
(.6-1.3 cm)

Low elevation
Occasional

*head*

Jessie M. Harris

This low-growing plant can be overlooked, even in full bloom. It frequently grows in clumps, sometimes forming a mat of plants. Most leaves are at the base of the plant and are gray-green and spoon-shaped. There are several flower heads in a tight cluster at the top of the stem. The heads are so compact and the flowers so small that they appear to be in bud even when blooming. Solitary pussy toes (*A. solitaria*) has a single flower head. Plantain-leaved pussy toes (*A. plantaginfolia*) has three-veined leaves. Catfoots (*Gnaphalium spp.*) resemble pussy toes, but have much leafier stems.

This is a food plant for the larvae of American painted lady butterfly (*Vanessa virginiensis*).

◆ **HABITAT**—Open woods and dry ground.
◆ **LOCATIONS**—Cooper Road Trail, Rich Mountain Road.
◆ **BLOOMS MARCH - MAY**

# Carolina Vetch

*Vicia caroliniana*

Pea Family
(*Fabaceae*)

Plant: sprawling or
climbing stems up
to 3′ in length
(.9 m)
Flower: ½″
(1.3 cm)

Low-mid elevation
Frequent

Harry Ellis

5-petaled Pea
family flower

Of the four species of vetch found in the park, Carolina is the only native species and the most common. This plant is usually sprawling over the ground or climbing on other plants. There are 7-20 white flowers (sometimes the bottom "keel" petals are bluish) in each loose floral cluster. The stamens are held within the keel petals and spring upward to dust pollinating insects when the petals are opened by a visitor. The compound leaves are densely hairy and are arranged alternately on the stem. Each leaf is divided into 10-18 leaflets, and the terminal (end) leaflet is modified into a tendril.

Like most other members of the Pea family, this species improves the soil by adding nitrogen to it.

◆ **HABITAT**—Woods, borders, and thickets.

◆ **LOCATIONS**—Rich Mountain Road, Schoolhouse Gap Trail.

◆ **BLOOMS  APRIL - JUNE**

# BEAKED DODDER, LOVE-VINE

*Cuscuta
rostrata*

Dodder Family
(*Cuscutaceae*)

Plant: 3'-4'
(.9-1.2 m.)
Flower: ⅛"-¼"
(0.3-0.6 cm)

Wide range
Frequent

Harry Ellis

Beaked Dodder is an odd plant indeed. The orange, yarn-like stems twining around neighboring plants creates a scene from a science fiction movie. In fact, this dodder was described in an early park wildflower book as a plant the Smokies would be better off without. Its lack of popularity can be attributed to its parasitic nature; the orange stems are without chlorophyll, the green pigment that helps plants manufacture food from sunlight. Without chlorophyll, beaked dodder must attach itself to a host plant, from which it derives energy, nutrients, and water. Beaked dodder stems bear clusters of tiny white, lobed, bell-shaped flowers. There are no leaves or roots.

The Cherokee called this plant "Love-in-a-tangle."

◆ HABITAT—Fields, open woods, and thickets.
◆ LOCATIONS—Cades Cove Loop Road, Kanati Fork Trail.
◆ BLOOMS AUGUST - OCTOBER

# WILD SARSAPARILLA

*Aralia nudicaulis*

Ginseng Family
(*Araliaceae*)

Plant: 8"-16"
(2-4 dm)
Flower: ½"-1¾"
inches diameter
(12-40 mm)

Mid-high elevation
Occasional

Rob and Ann Simpson

There are several unrelated plants which all bear the common name "sarsaparilla." The reason so many plants in different families share the same moniker is that their roots have the same "root beer" odor. The species found in the park is a member of the Ginseng family. The long, twisted, fleshy, underground stem (rhizome) can be used to make tea (park plants are protected, however). From this rhizome, two stalks arise. The stalk devoted to leaves is the taller, 8"-16" (2-4 dm). The leaf is doubly compound—3 main divisions, each division with 5 leaflets. The flowering stalk is smooth, leafless, typically 6"-12" (1.5- 3 dm) tall, and terminates in 3 (rarely 2-7) many-flowered umbels. Individual flowers are small and have 5 greenish-white petals. The fruit is a small black berry that ripens in the early fall.

◆ **HABITAT**—Upland woodlands; dry, rocky ridgetops.
◆ **BLOOMS MAY - JUNE**

# NODDING POGONIA

Orchid Family
*(Orchidaceae)*

Plant: 4″-12″
(1-3 dm)
Flower: 1″
(2.5 cm)

Low-mid elevations
Occasional

Joseph G. Strauch, Jr.

The stem of this orchid is succulent, tinged with maroon, and usually less than 8″ (20 cm) tall. The plant typically has only a few leaves, and they are arranged alternately on the stem. Despite the scientific name, *Triphora*, literally, "three-bearing," the plant can have from 1-6 flowers. Even if there are exactly three, it is rare to find all in bloom simultaneously. The sepals and lateral petals are white to pale purple.

If you see nodding pogonia in bloom, consider yourself extremely lucky. The plant spends several years growing underground, storing food and energy until conditions for flowering are optimal. Then, even when it does bloom, each flower lasts only a day or two. This orchid derives most of its nutrition from decaying matter in the soil.

♦ **HABITAT**—Damp rich woods (particularly hemlock forests), frequently on rotting logs.

♦ BLOOMS JULY - SEPTEMBER

119

# SPRING-BEAUTY

*Claytonia caroliniana*

Purslane Family
(*Portulacaceae*)

Plant: 2"-12"
(5-30 cm)
Flower: ½"-¾"
(1.3-1.9 cm)

Wide range
Common

Charles K. Webb

Glorious masses of this early spring wildflower adorn the forest floor even before the trees leaf out. The blossoms only open when the sun shines, which is when pollinating insects are more likely to be about. The delicate flowers have five petals that are either white or pale pink with darker pink veining. A pair of oval, dark green leaves are present about halfway up the stem. A closely related species, narrow-leaved spring-beauty (*C. virginica*), is very similar except the leaves are linear and longer. *C. virginica* is more common at the lower elevations while *C. caroliniana* is more common higher up.

The starchy tubers of spring-beauty are eaten by black bears as well as non-native wild hogs.

◆ **HABITAT**—Moist woods.
◆ **LOCATIONS**—Clingmans Dome Road, Chestnut Top Trail.
◆ BLOOMS MARCH - MAY

Wood-sorrel Family
(*Oxalidaceae*)

Plant: 2"-6"
(5-15 cm)
Flower: ½"-¾"
(1.3-1.9 cm)

High elevation
Common

*cleistogamous
flower*

Connie Toops

The small white blossoms etched with pink lines look very much like the common spring-beauty. However, the season of bloom and leaves will allow you to easily distinguish the two. Wood-sorrel is a summer-blooming plant with distinctive shamrock-like leaves.

Wood-sorrel flower stems have three, two-lobed leaves. Below the leaves is another flower. This cleistogamous (closed) flower has developed to insure seed production. It self-pollinates and produces an alternate set of seeds to those of the showy flowers. Such seeds, however, lack the genetic variation of seeds from open flowers. The generic name "*Oxalis*" refers to the content of oxalic acid in the leaves. This chemical makes apples sour and wood-sorrels taste bitter.

◆ **HABITAT**—Rich spruce-fir and northern hardwood forests.
◆ **LOCATIONS**—Clingmans Dome Road, Forney Ridge Trail.
◆ BLOOMS JUNE - JULY

# WILD GERANIUM

*Geranium maculatum*

Geranium Family
(*Geraniaceae*)

Plant: 1'-2½'
(.3-.75 m)
Flower: 1"-1½"
(2.5-3.8 cm)

Low-mid elevation
Common

Harry Ellis

The bright pink to purple blossoms of this plant make it easy to identify from a distance. Closer inspection of the five petals reveal fine lines leading toward the reproductive parts. In the 1700s, a botanist first theorized that bees use these to find the flower's nectar. If we could see the same ultraviolet light spectrum that bees do, we would find these "nectar guides" are truly bold markers.

To insure cross-pollination, the single pistil matures a day or two after the 10 stamens. A seed capsule develops 3-5 weeks later. This beaked fruit gives us the name geranium from the Greek *geranos* (a crane). The "geranium" of home gardens is in the same plant family but a different genus (*Pelargonium*).

◆ **HABITAT**—Rich, moist woods and coves.

◆ **LOCATIONS**—Newfound Gap Road, Porters Creek Trail.

◆ BLOOMS APRIL - MAY

*Dicentra eximia*

Fumitory Family
(*Fumariaceae*)

Plant: 10"-18"
(25-45 cm)
Flower: ¾"
(2 cm)

Low-mid elevation
Scarce

Bill Lea

Bleeding heart could not have been better named. Its small pink blossoms rise above a cluster of delicately cut basal leaves. The blossom is a fusion of four petals into a heart-shaped flower. Two larger, outer petals form the heart, giving us the genus name, *Dicentra*, Greek for "two-spurred." The smaller, often darker, inner petals resemble a drop of blood falling from the flower. The plant is most often found in small groups. Bees, butterflies, and even hummingbirds pollinate it.

This is perhaps the rarest and most beautiful of the three members of its family found in the Smokies. Squirrel corn and Dutchman's britches can be easily distinguished from bleeding heart by the latter's pink blossoms.

◆ **HABITAT**—Rich, moist woods, streambanks.
◆ **LOCATIONS**—Roaring Fork Motor Nature Tr., Cosby Nature Tr.
◆ BLOOMS APRIL - JUNE

# CLIMBING FUMITORY

*Adlumia fungosa*

Fumitory Family
(*Fumariaceae*)

Plant: Climbing or
clambering, stems
up to 4 yds long
(4 m)

Flower: ¼″ wide;
½″ long
(5 mm wide,
15 mm long)

Low-mid elevation
Rare

Jessie M. Harris

Consider yourself lucky to spot climbing fumitory, for although the geographic range of this wildflower is large (Quebec to Minnesota, then southward to North Carolina and Tennessee), nowhere is it very common. Look for it clambering and twining on other plants in moist coves, rock outcrops, and areas that have been recently burned. The foliage (compound leaves arranged alternately on the fragile stems) is delicate and wispy, hence the common name "fumitory," *fumus* + *terrae*, "smoke of the earth." Fumitory flowers are very similar to those of bleeding heart (*Dicentra*). The genus is dedicated to Major John Adlum (1759-1836), an amateur botanist, and *fungosa*, meaning spongy or mushroom-like, refers to the spongy texture of the petals.

◆ **HABITAT**—Moist coves and rock outcrops.
◆ **LOCATION**—Tremont Road.
◆ BLOOMS JUNE - SEPTEMBER

*Cypripedium acaule*

Orchid Family
(*Orchidaceae*)

Plant: 8"-16"
(20-40 cm)
Flower: 1"-2½"
(2.5-6.8 cm)

Low-mid elevation
Frequent

Bill Lea

For many, finding this plant in the wild is a memorable experience. The two large (4"-9" long, 1"-5" wide) basal leaves are strongly ribbed, pale beneath, and somewhat hairy. The distinctive lip petal is an inflated pouch—the "slipper."

This is our only lady's slipper without leaves on the flowering stalk. The generic name "*Cypripedium*" refers to Kupris (or Venus), the Greek goddess of love, and "pedilon" meaning "shoe." Like many orchids, pink lady's slipper is virtually impossible to propagate or to transplant. Extreme caution should be used when purchasing native orchids. Unscrupulous vendors dig these plants from the wild, even from national parks where digging plants is illegal. Pink lady's slipper should be enjoyed, undisturbed, in its natural setting.

◆ **HABITAT**—Dry woods, frequently under pines or oaks.

◆ BLOOMS APRIL - JULY

# PINK TURTLEHEAD

*Chelone lyonii*

Snapdragon Family
(*Scrophulariaceae*)

Plant: 1'-2'
(.3-.6 m)
Flower: 1"
(2.5 cm)

Wide range
Frequent

Betsy Strauch

*Chelone* is Greek for tortoise; an apt name for this plant. The pink to purple blossoms are one of nature's wonders. Five petals have fused into this two-lipped tube to "swallow" bees. The turtle's head is marked by yellow hairs on the lower three-lobed lip, perhaps acting as "landing lights" for aerial pollinators. When a bee pushes into the flower, the four fertile stamens place pollen onto its head and back. At the next flower, pollen is accepted by a single pistil.

The white turtlehead (*C. glabra*) is distinguished by its white flowers, nearly stemless leaves, and its restriction to low elevation. The pink turtlehead's leaves have obvious stems and rounded bases.

Pink turtlehead has been used to treat itching and worms.

◆ **HABITAT**—Seeps, stream banks, and spruce-fir forests.
◆ **LOCATIONS**—Clingmans Dome Road, The Boulevard Trail.
◆ BLOOMS JULY - SEPTEMBER

Orchid Family
(*Orchidaceae*)

Plant: 12"-15"
(30-38 cm)
Flower: 2"
(5 cm)

Low-mid elevation
Scarce

Jessie M. Harris

This native orchid gets its common name from the three greenish-maroon-brown sepals that spread upward above the flower. The two lateral petals, pink to white in color, face forward and form a tube over the lower lip. The lip is intricately colored—deep rose patch at the tip, yellow bristled crest in the throat, purple etched veins throughout. The plant usually has a single flower. There is a long leaf-like bract below the flower, and the plant's single leaf is halfway up the stem. This plant is very scarce in the southern Appalachians, so consider yourself very lucky to find it in bloom. Note its location, and report it to a ranger when you return from your hike.

◆ **HABITAT**—Well-drained, open hillsides often with blueberries and other heath family plants.
◆ **LOCATION**—Meigs Creek Trail.
◆ BLOOMS MAY - JULY

# SHOWY ORCHIS

*Galearis spectabilis*

Orchid Family
(*Orchidaceae*)

Plant: 5"-10"
(13-25 cm)
Flower: 1"
(2.5 cm)

Low-mid elevation
Common

Jessie M. Harris

This spectacularly attractive orchid occurs in a wide range of habitats, from rich woods to disturbed road and trail edges. The two (sometimes three) basal leaves are 3"-8" long, egg-shaped, and lustrous. The flowering stalk bears 2-12 flowers. While the flowering stalk has no true leaves, a long leaf-like bract is found at the base of each flower. Each flower is about 1" long, with a pink or lilac hood and a white lip. The lip is a landing platform for pollinating insects that push their way through the hood. The backward-pointing spur is a rich nectar source that the pollinators cannot resist.

Surely showy orchis is one of the Smokies' loveliest wildflowers. Enjoy it in the wild—these orchids do not survive in home gardens.

◆ **HABITAT**—Rich, moist woods and trailsides.

◆ **LOCATIONS**—Roaring Fork M.N.T., Lower Mt. Cammerer Trail.

◆ BLOOMS APRIL - MAY

# GOAT'S RUE

Pea Family
*(Fabaceae)*

Plant: 7"-28"
(2-7 dm)
Flower: ½"
(15 mm)

Low-mid elevation
Frequent

Jessie M. Harris

Goat's rue is well adapted to dry, open places. Its long taproot enables it to resist drought, and silky whitish hairs covering stem and leaflets retard waterloss. The stiff, erect stem rarely branches, but if it does so, it will be from the base of the plant. The leaves are arranged alternately on the stem. The upper flower petal (termed the "standard") is creamy white to lemon yellow; the lower petals ("keels" and lateral "wings") are rose pink. The seeds are borne in a densely hairy pod that is 1" - 2" (2.5-5.5 cm) long. Quail eat the seeds. However, the plant contains chemicals that are toxic to humans, mites, insects and fish. Tephrosin and rotenone are used in minute quantities to treat tumors; in larger quantities these same chemicals are employed as pesticides and to kill fish and other aquatic organisms.

◆ **HABITAT**—Open woods, outcrops, barrens, clearings.
◆ BLOOMS MAY - JUNE

129

# HAIRY BEARD-TONGUE

*Penstemon canescens*

Snapdragon Family
(*Scrophulariaceae*)

Plant: 1'-2'
(.3-.6 m)
Flower: 1"-1½"
(2.5-3.8 cm)

Low-mid elevation
Frequent

Bill Lea

*flower
cross-section*

Hairy is the perfect description of this plant. The stem, the leaves, and even one of the stamens are covered with thin, glandular hairs. The "bearded tongue" is a sterile (anther-less) filament covered with yellow hairs. It lies upon the floor of the two-lipped flower. Four fertile stamens hang above; ready to deposit pollen on any insect which enters the flower. The tubular blossom is formed from five fused petals. These violet-purple to pinkish (rarely white) petals have nectar guide lines of contrasting colors.

Hairy beard-tongue has a circular cluster of leaves at its base and opposite, short-stemmed or stemless leaves along the stem. At the flower head, the leaves clasp the stem.

◆ **HABITAT**—Dry woods, rocky areas.
◆ **LOCATIONS**—Laurel Creek Road, Chestnut Top Trail.
◆ BLOOMS MAY - JULY

*Desmodium
nudiflorum*

Pea Family
*(Fabaceae)*

Plant: 1'-3'
(.3-.9 m)
Flower: under ½"
(0.5 cm)

Low-mid elevation
Common

Hugh Nourse

There are 14 species of tick-trefoil in the park. Naked-flowered tick-trefoil's flowering stalk arises from the base of the plant and is leafless ("naked"). The sticky, hairy seed pods have 2-4 joints. The stem bearing the foliage (separate from the flower stalk) is usually only 1'-2' tall. The compound leaves crowd at the summit and have three leaflets. The end leaflet is distinctly longer than wide. Whorled tick-trefoil (*D. glutinosum*) has a leafy flowering stalk, its seed pods have shorter stalks (¼"-½" long), and the end leaflet is about as wide as long.

Don't worry about getting ticks—the common name refers to the seed pods, which cling like ticks.

◆ **HABITAT**—Woodlands.
◆ **LOCATIONS**—Rich Mountain Road, Schoolhouse Gap Trail.
◆ BLOOMS JULY - AUGUST

# ROSE TWISTED-STALK

*Streptopus roseus*

Lily Family
*(Liliaceae)*

Plant: 12″-24″
(30-61 cm)
Flower: ½″
(1.3 cm)

Mid-high elevation
Frequent

Jessie M. Harris

This lovely plant is named for its twisted flower stalk. It twists around the stem from its point of origin opposite the leaf, so that the flower ends up under the leaf. The lance-shaped leaves may be up to 6″ long with distinct parallel veins and minute hairs along the leaf edges. The rosy to deep pink flowers are tubular, while the tips of the tiny petals curve back as they age. Less common, up to a foot taller, and found only at higher elevations in the park is another twisted-stalk (*S. amplexifolius*). This is a larger plant with greenish-white flowers and leaf bases that completely surround the stem.

Rose twisted-stalk follows the spruce-fir and Northern hardwood forests north to Canada and is near its southern limit in the park.

◆ **HABITAT**—Moist woods.
◆ **LOCATIONS**—Newfound Gap Road, The Boulevard Trail.
◆ BLOOMS APRIL - JUNE

132

# FALSE DRAGONHEAD

*Physostegia virginiana*

Mint Family
*(Lamiaceae)*

Plant: 6″-5′
(.2 -1.5 m)
Flower: 1″-1½″
(2.5-4 cm)

Low elevation
Scarce

Jessie M. Harris

This plant's alternate common name (obedient) comes from the fact that you can gently twirl a flower around the stalk, and it will remain in place, obedient to your command. The pink to lavender (rarely white) flowers are funnel-shaped, and distinctly 2-lipped. The upper lip is erect and nearly entire, while the lower lip is 3-parted, the middle lobe broad and notched. Four stamens arching under the upper lip dust an insect with pollen as it crawls through the inch-long flower tube to the nectary gland at the rear. Flowers are arranged in a terminal spike that can be quite long (4″-8″ on a robust plant), so one plant may have dozens of flowers. Like all mints, false dragonhead has a square stem and opposite leaves, but it is not particularly fragrant.

◆ **HABITAT**—Grassy balds and semi-open moist-wet habitats.
◆ **LOCATION**—Ace Gap Trail.
◆ BLOOMS JULY - OCTOBER

# SMALL PURPLE-FRINGED ORCHID

Bill Lea

*Platanthera psycodes*

Orchid Family
(*Orchidaceae*)

Plant: 1'-2½'
(0.3-0.8 m)
Flower: ½" with spur of
equal length
(1.3 cm)

High elevation
Occasional

*dumbbell-shaped tube*

One of the prettiest of our summer orchids, this plant can be quickly identified by the tall cluster (to 8") of lilac to pinkish-purple blossoms. It is sometimes called butterfly orchid, because the flower's lower lip has three deeply fringed lobes and thus resembles a resting butterfly. A look into the throat of the blossom will reveal a dumbbell-shaped tube leading back to the hidden nectary in the petal spur.
The stout stem supports 1-5 deep green leaves up to 9" long.

The similar, larger purple-fringed orchid (*P. grandiflora*) has a longer (to 10") and wider (6") flower cluster. It has an oval tube leading to the nectary. The purple fringeless orchid (*P. peramoena*) is a low elevation species with flowers which lack the deeply-cut fringe.

◆ **HABITAT**—Grassy balds and high elevation roadsides.
◆ **LOCATIONS**—Clingmans Dome Road, Forney Creek Trail.
◆ BLOOMS JUNE - AUGUST

*Vernonia noveboracensis*

Aster Family
(*Asteraceae*)

Plant: 3'-6'
(0.9-1.8 m)
Flower head: ½"-
¾" (1.3-1.9 cm)

Low elevations
Scarce

Harry Ellis

New York ironweed is a tall wildflower—up to 6' at maturity. This robust aster has a dozen or more deep purple flower heads in a branched cluster. Green, leafy bracts with thread-like tips enclose the base of each head. Each head is composed of 30-50 individual flowers. The lance-shaped leaves are toothed, alternate, 3"-10" long, and virtually stalkless. Tall ironweed (*V. gigantea*), also found in the park, has fewer (15-30) flowers in each head and bracts with blunt tips.

This plant is spectacular in bloom, especially when sharing a meadow with the late summer goldenrods. The combination of bright purple and sunny yellow make for some of the most vivid wildflower colors of the year.

◆ **HABITAT**—Wet meadows.
◆ **LOCATIONS**—Cades Cove Loop Road.
◆ BLOOMS JULY - SEPTEMBER

# PALE MEADOW BEAUTY

*Rhexia mariana*

Meadow Beauty Family
(*Melastomataceae*)

Plant: 4"-3'
(0.1-1 m)
Flower: 1"
(2 cm)

Low-mid elevation
Rare

Jessie M. Harris

*fruit*

There are two "meadow beauties" in the Great Smokies, so look carefully to determine which species you have found. Pale meadow beauty's stem is nearly circular in cross-section and lacks wings. Meadow beauty's (*R. virginica*) stem, in contrast, is angular (almost square in cross-section) with conspicuous wings, particularly in the middle portion of the stem. Meadow beauty has leaves that are 1"-2" long (2-6 cm), and ⅜"-1⅛" (1-3 cm) wide. The leaves of pale meadow beauty are just as long, but much narrower.

The fruit is an urn-shaped capsule that is covered with gland-tipped hairs. These persistent capsules are so distinctive that it is easy to identify these plants in mid-winter, long after petals and leaves have withered.

◆ **HABITAT**—bogs and low meadows.

◆ **LOCATION**—Cades Cove meadows.

◆ BLOOMS MAY - OCTOBER

*Liparis lilifolia*

# LILY-LEAVED TWAYBLADE

Orchid Family
(*Orchidaceae*)

Plant: 4"-12"
(1-3 dm)
Flower: About 1"
(2.5 cm)

Low elevations
Infrequent

*flower*

Jessie M. Harris

Lily-leaved twayblade is an orchid whose leaves are present when it flowers. The basal leaves are lustrous, oval or elliptic in shape, 2"-6" (5-15 cm) long, and about half that wide. Note the prominent keel on the underside of the leaves. The stem is leafless and usually about 6" (15 cm) high. The flowers extend along the top half of the slender stem. It may take several weeks to complete the flowering of all the buds, from bottom to top, on a single plant. The loose raceme has 5 to 30 flowers. The lip of the flower is a broad, mauve-colored, inviting landing platform for insect pollinators. "*Liparos*" means fat and alludes to the shining, greasy-looking leaves. Lily-leaved twayblade is widespread over eastern North America, ranging from Ontario westward to Minnesota, then southward to Arkansas and Georgia.

◆ **HABITAT**— Moist forests, floodplains, rich woods and stream banks.
◆ BLOOMS MAY - JULY

# Fringed Polygala, Gay-wings

Jessie M. Harris

*Polygala paucifolia*

Milkwort Family
*Polygalaceae*

Plant: 2"-6"
(5-15 cm)
Flower: ¾"
(20 mm)

Low elevation
Infrequent

Due to the unusual structure of the fringed polygala flower, you might mistake it for an orchid or a legume. Many plants in the Milkwort family have tiny flowers, but the distinctive structure of the corolla (petals) and calyx (sepals) are readily observable in the large, showy fringed polygala flower. Each plant will have 1-5 flowers at the tips of the branches. The corolla is composed of 3 petals that are partially fused into a tube. The lowest petal ("keel") is fringed at the tip. Insect pollinators use this as a landing pad. The calyx is composed of 5 sepals: the upper and 2 lowest sepals are of modest size, while the 2 lateral sepals ("wings") are large, colored, and strongly resemble petals. The species name, *paucifolia*, means "few leaves" in Greek.

◆ **HABITAT**—Moist forests.
◆ **LOCATION**—Abrams Falls Trail.
◆ BLOOMS APRIL - JUNE

138

*Aquilegia canadensis*

Buttercup Family
(*Ranunculaceae*)

Plant: 1'-2½'
(.3-.75 m)
Flower: 1"-2"
(2.5-5 cm)

Low-mid elevation
Frequent

Adam Jones

With its yellow and red flowers hanging from a slender stalk, the columbine is both bold and delicate. Its five red sepals drape over the yellow blade of the five petals. Together these circle a cluster of dangling stamens. Long red petal spurs rise above the flower and form nectaries. Hummingbirds are best suited to pollinate this blossom. Their long tongues and hovering ability allow them to reap the hidden nectar high up in the petals. They must, however, brush past the pistil as the stamens dust their tiny foreheads with pollen.

Sometimes columbine is called rock bells for its habitat. It was once suggested this be our national wildflower because of its resemblance to eagle talons. *Aquilegia* is Latin for eagle.

◆ **HABITAT**—Moist, rocky areas.
◆ **LOCATIONS**—Laurel Creek Road, Thomas Divide Trail.
◆ **BLOOMS APRIL - JUNE**

# FIRE PINK

*Silene virginica*

Pink Family
(*Caryophyllaceae*)

Plant: 1'-2'
(.3-.6 m)
Flower: 1 ½" wide
(3.7 cm)

Wide range
Frequent

Connie Toops

One look and you'll ask, "who called this brilliant red flower pink?" "Pink" refers not to the color of the petals, but to their shape. Each of the five petals is pinked or notched at its tip. A loose cluster of star-shaped flowers sit atop a stem with pairs of slender opposite leaves.

Sometimes this plant is known as "catchfly" because it has sticky hairs on its fused sepals. This tubular calyx protects the flower's nectar from crawling insects. The deep tubular corolla evolved to use flying insects and hummingbirds as its primary pollinators. These animals have a better chance of passing pollen to another flower than crawling insects, especially in this plant's harsh habitat where few plants grow very near each other.

◆ **HABITAT**—Dry, rocky slopes, including roadsides.
◆ **LOCATIONS**—Little River Road, Chestnut Top Trail.
◆ **BLOOMS APRIL - JUNE**

## *Trillium erectum*

Harry Ellis

# WAKE ROBIN

Lily Family
(*Liliaceae*)

Plant: 8"-16"
(20-41 cm)
Flower: 2½"
(6 cm)

Mid-high elevation
Frequent

$S$pring may begin when this trillium blooms, as its appearance is supposed to wake up the robins. The color of the flower is highly variable. It's usually purple or maroon, but don't be surprised if you occasionally see varieties colored green, pale cream, or white. A single flower overtops the whorl of three leaves at the summit of the stem. After the petals fall off the plant, a conspicuous, oval red berry forms. A whiff of the odor given off by this perennial will give you an indication why its other common names include "stinking willie," "stinking Benjamin," and "wet dog trillium." This foul odor, described by some as "disgustingly fishy," is apparently attractive to the carrion-feeding flies which pollinate this species.

◆ **HABITAT**—Moist woods.

◆ **LOCATIONS**—Greenbrier Road, Lower Mount Cammerer Trail.

◆ **BLOOMS APRIL - MAY**

# VASEY'S TRILLIUM

*Trillium vaseyi*

Lily Family
*(Liliaceae)*

Plant: 8″-20″
(20-50 cm)
Flower: 2″-4″
(5-10 cm)

Low-mid elevation
Frequent

Connie Toops

Largest of the North American trilliums, this spectacular species is also the latest blooming. The pleasant-smelling flowers burst forth in late spring to nod below the three-leaved whorl. The stalked flower is a study in contrasts with the bright green sepals encircling the deep maroon or red petals. The pollen-bearing anthers at the tips of the six stamens are white with a dark stripe. The flowers can be huge—sometimes 4″ across! Plant parts in threes and multiples of three are a characteristic of the lily family. Trilliums are easily identified by the arrangement of three whorled leaves, three sepals and three petals.

Named for naturalist George Vasey (1822-1893), this plant lives only in the southern Appalachians.

♦ **HABITAT**—Moist woods.

♦ **LOCATIONS**—Roaring Fork Motor Nature Tr., Bradley Fork Tr.

♦ **BLOOMS APRIL - MAY**

*Spigelia marilandica*

Logania Family
(*Loganiaceae*)

Plant: 12"-24"
(30-61 cm)
Flower: 1" wide
1"-2" long
(2.5-5 cm)

Low elevation
Scarce

Jessie M. Harris

Although this plant is scarce in the park, it is conspicuous if you are fortunate enough to find it in bloom. The flowers are vivid red and tubular in shape. The tips of the five pointed petals flare slightly backwards to reveal an equally vivid yellow interior. Indian pink has 4-7 pairs of leaves.

There are no other members of the Logania family in the southern Appalachians, but all plants in this family, including Indian pink, serve as a source of the poison strychnine. Cherokees and later European settlers used extracts of Indian pink roots as a treatment for intestinal parasites.

◆ **HABITAT**—Rich, moist woods and thickets. Usually on "sweet" (limestone bedrock) soil.

◆ **LOCATIONS**—Rich Mountain Road, Scott Mountain Trail.

◆ **BLOOMS APRIL - JUNE**

# CARDINAL FLOWER

*Lobelia cardinalis*

Bellflower Family
(*Campanulaceae*)

Plant: 2'-4'
(.6-1.2 m)
Flower:1"-1½"
(2.5-3.8 cm)

Low-mid elevation
Frequent

Jessie M. Harris

This wildflower gets its common name from the resemblance of the brilliant red flowers to the crimson robes worn by Roman Catholic cardinals. The blossoms are arranged in a loose spike, each flower on a short stalk. The leaves are veiny, coarsely toothed, and arranged alternately along the stem. A basal rosette of leaves is green year-round. Great blue lobelia (*L. siphilitica*) resembles cardinal flower in growth form and habitat, but its blossoms are blue.

Cardinal flower has become a popular garden plant. Its striking blossoms are attractive to butterflies and hummingbirds. Along streams, periodic flooding clears debris from the plant, allowing year-round photosynthesis by the basal leaves.

◆ **HABITAT**—Streamside thickets, wet roadsides.
◆ **LOCATIONS**—Tremont Road, Schoolhouse Gap Trail.
◆ **BLOOMS JULY - OCTOBER**

144

# Monarda didyma

Mint Family
*(Lamiaceae)*

Plant: 2'-4'
(0.6-1.2 m)
Flower: 1"-1½"
(2.5-3.8 cm)

Wide range
Frequent

Harry Ellis

Bee-balm is a feast for the eyes and nose. Its striking red flowers in dense heads are attractive to bees, butterflies, and hummingbirds. Two pollen-containing stamens protrude from each flower. Like many mints, bee-balm has a square stem and opposite leaves. The foliage is pungent, and the leaves below the flower head may be tinged with red. The leaves have stems, are hairy along the veins, and have serrated edges. Other Monardas found in the park are purple bee-balm (*Monarda media*—deep red-purple flowers), Horse-mint (*Monarda clinopodia*—whitish bracts and flowers), and wild bergamot (*Monarda fistulosa*—lilac flowers and pinkish bracts).

This wildflower has become a popular garden plant.

- **HABITAT**—Rich, moist woods.
- **LOCATIONS**—Clingmans Dome Road, Kanati Fork Trail.
- **BLOOMS JULY - OCTOBER**

# BUTTERFLY-WEED

*Asclepias tuberosa*

Milkweed Family
(*Asclepiadaceae*)

Plant: 1'-2'
(.3-.6 m)
Flower: ½"
(1.3 cm)

Low-mid elevation
Occasional

Harry Ellis

This is perhaps the only milkweed without milky sap. It may also be the most beautiful. A rich cluster of deep orange blossoms cover this plant in summer. The individual flowers are composed of five drooping petals with a crown above. The crown is created as a trap for flying insects. As an insect searches for nectar, its leg may slip into a small slit between anthers. If it is strong enough to extract its foot, it will also drag out a saddlebag-like structure containing pollen. Only the strong (butterflies and bees) are capable of carrying so much pollen to another plant.

Butterfly-weed is sometimes called chigger-weed, perhaps because the biting mite shares the same habitat.

◆ **HABITAT**—Roadsides, dry woods, and fields.
◆ **LOCATIONS**—Cades Cove Loop Road, Abrams Creek Trail.
◆ BLOOMS MAY - AUGUST

Lily Family
*(Liliaceae)*

Plant: 3'-8'
(0.9-2.7 m)
Flower: 5" wide
(13 cm)

Wide range
Common

Bill Lea

This spectacular member of the lily family is one of the showiest wildflowers in the park. There may be over two dozen large, nodding flowers per plant. The petals and sepals turn sharply back on themselves, giving the impression of the caps worn by ancient Turks. Green streaks appear at the base of each floral segment such that a "star" is formed in the middle of each flower where the nectar bearing glands are positioned. Also native to the park is a smaller lily with a more southerly range called Carolina lily (*L. michauxii*). This species does not have the central green star, and its leaves taper to a blunt point, unlike the Turk's cap lily, whose leaves are more sharply pointed. Carolina lily is also found on drier sites.

◆ **HABITAT**—Moist woods, balds, trailside thickets.
◆ **LOCATIONS**—Newfound Gap Road, Kanati Fork Trail.
◆ **BLOOMS JULY - SEPTEMBER**

# ORANGE JEWELWEED

*Impatiens capensis*

Touch-me-not
Family
(*Balsaminaceae*)

Plant: 2'-5'
(0.6-1.5 m)
Flower: 1"
(2.5 cm)

Wide range
Common

Adam Jones

This tall succulent plant with simple, round-toothed leaves has unmistakable flowers. Numerous orange, spotted blooms dangle from fine stalks like precious jewels. Orange jewelweed is very similar to pale jewelweed (*I. pallida*) which grows in the same habitat. Flower coloration is enough to distinguish the two.

Hummingbirds, butterflies and bees are attracted to this flower. The circular petals force pollinators to push past either the mature stamens, which deposit white pollen on them, or the small green pistil, which receives pollen. To avoid self-pollination, the flower is first male then female. The name jewelweed refers to the way water beads up on its leaves.

- ◆ **HABITAT**—Moist areas.
- ◆ **LOCATIONS**—Roaring Fork Motor Nature Tr., Little River Tr.
- ◆ BLOOMS JUNE - SEPTEMBER

*Platanthera
ciliaris*

Orchid Family
(*Orchidaceae*)

Plant: 10"-24"
(25-60 cm)
Flower: ¾"
(2 cm)

Low-mid elevation
Common

Bill Lea

This beautiful orchid is unforgettable. The blossoms can range in color from bright yellow to deep orange. Most commonly, the blossoms are a delicate orange, which some enthusiasts call "sherbet" or "Creamsicle" orange. The blossoms grow in a cylindrical spike that is 2"-6" long and 2" wide. The bottom lip of the blossom is conspicuously fringed. The plant's basal leaves are large (up to 6" long, 2" wide), but the upper leaves are much smaller.

Orchid seeds are tiny, almost dust-like. The seeds have no nutrient stores and so form associations with a particular species of fungus for germination and early growth. It is this "mycorrhizal" relationship that makes orchids difficult to germinate or transplant.

◆ **HABITAT**—Dry woods and thickets.
◆ **LOCATIONS**—Cades Cove Loop Road, Fork Ridge Trail.
◆ BLOOMS JULY - SEPTEMBER

# EARLY YELLOW VIOLET

*Viola rotundifolia*

Violet Family
(*Violaceae*)

Plant: 1½"-5"
(4-13 cm)
Flower: ½"-¾"
(1.3-1.9 cm)

Wide range
Common

Harry Ellis

This yellow violet blooms in early spring, sometimes before its leaves appear. The flower has usually bloomed and faded by the time spring woodland wildflowers peak in the Great Smokies (about mid-April). The leaves have an unmistakable heart-shape with beautifully scalloped margins. After the flowers fade, the leaves continue to expand, usually lying flat on the ground. The leaves become "rotund," as the specific name suggests, measuring up to 5" by summer's end.

Because leaves are absent from the flower's stalk, this is considered one of the "stemless" violets. It is the only yellow stemless violet found in the park. The three lower petals have brown veins to guide nectar-seeking insects to the spurred petal.

◆ **HABITAT**—Rich woods.
◆ **LOCATIONS**—Roaring Fork Motor Nature Tr., Kanati Fork Tr.
◆ BLOOMS MARCH - APRIL

Lily Family
(*Liliaceae*)

Plant: 4"-10"
(10-25 cm)
Flower: 1"-1½"
(2.5-3.8 cm)

Wide range
Common

Ken Voorhis

This familiar spring wildflower is often found in large patches which bloom before the trees leaf out. The nodding, solitary flower rises above the long, elliptic, paired leaves which are conspicuously mottled. These markings are responsible for the common name, which some thought resembled brook trout. The recurved petals and sepals are the same size and color.

The small, toothed bulbs have spawned the other common name for this species, dogtooth violet. Like many woodland wildflowers, this species has slow growth and low reproduction. It may take seven or more years to flower.

◆ **HABITAT**—Moist hardwood forests.

◆ **LOCATIONS**—Roaring Fork Motor Nature Trail, Cove Hardwood Nature Trail.

◆ **BLOOMS MARCH - MAY**

# Smooth Yellow Violet

*Jessie M. Harris*

*Viola pubescens
var. leiocarpon*

Violet Family
(Violaceae)

Plant: 4"-12"
(10-30 cm)
Flower: ½"-¾"
(1.3-2 cm)

Low-mid elevation
Frequent

*cleistogamous
flowers*

Smooth yellow violet is a member of the "stemmed" violets, its leaves alternate along a stem on which the stalked flowers are also borne. This species is often hairless, as the common name implies. Its flowers sit atop long stems held high above the stem leaves. Smooth yellow violet usually has more than one kidney-shaped leaf at the base of the plant.

Many violets can produce two kinds of flowers. In this species, after the prominent yellow-petaled ones are produced, inconspicuous cleistogamous colorless flowers may form, often near the base of the plant. These flowers never open, lack conspicuous petals, and are self-fertilized. The yellow flowers are pollinated by bees and butterflies.

◆ **HABITAT**—Moist woods.
◆ **LOCATIONS**—Little River Road, Huskey Gap Trail.
◆ BLOOMS APRIL-MAY

# HALBERD-LEAVED VIOLET

Violet Family
*(Violaceae)*

Plant: 4"-10"
(10-25 cm)
Flower: ½"-1"
(1.3-2.5 cm)

Low-mid elevation
Common

Jessie M. Harris

This yellow violet is one of the "stemmed" violets because its leaves are borne along an above ground stem. It is an early bloomer with easy to recognize arrowhead shaped leaves. These leaves (2-4) are clustered near the top of the stem; the silvery blotches on the upper surface of the leaves will help you spot this plant throughout the summer, after the flowers have faded.

This is one of the first spring wildflowers to bloom in the Great Smokies. Its specific name, *hastata*, means "spear-shaped," which refers to the leaf of this plant. A halberd was a tall battle ax type weapon used in the 15th and 16th centuries. The shape of the weapon's head was the inspiration for this violet's common name.

◆ **HABITAT**—Moist, mixed deciduous woods.
◆ **LOCATIONS**—Greenbrier Road, Porters Creek Trail.
◆ BLOOMS MARCH - MAY

# DWARF CINQUEFOIL

*Potentilla canadensis*

Rose Family
(*Rosaceae*)

Plant: 2"-6"
(5-15 cm)
Flower: ½"-⅔"
(1.3-1.7 cm)

Wide Range
Frequent

Greene Photo Services

Sometimes closely related species are hard to differentiate. Such is the case with the dwarf and common (*P. simplex*) cinquefoils. Both have five leaflets per leaf and flowers of five small yellow petals above a ring of five green sepals (hence the name cinquefoil). The best clue to accurate identification is that dwarf cinquefoil blossoms arise from the axil of the lowest leaf. In common cinquefoil, the first bloom comes from the axil of the second leaf.

This is a low-growing plant that can form mats by vegetative reproduction. Common cinquefoil leaves tend to be slightly larger than those of dwarf cinquefoil and have teeth below the middle. Common cinquefoil also prefers moister habitats.

- **HABITAT**—Dry open woods, balds, and fields.
- **LOCATIONS**—Rich Mountain Road, Kanati Fork Trail.
- BLOOMS APRIL - JUNE

*Hypericum graveolens*

St. John's-wort Family *(Clusiaceae)*

Plant: 1'-2'
(.3-6 m)
Flower: 1-1½"
(2.5-3.8 cm)

High elevation
Occasional

Jessie M. Harris

Mountain St. Johns-wort bears bright yellow flowers smelling sweetly of butterscotch. In fact, the specific name, *graveolens*, means "heavy-scented" in Greek. The flat-topped cluster of flowers of this plant may contain as few as four flowers or as many as 14. Mountain St. John's-wort has opposite, blunt-tipped leaves. A similar-looking plant, Mitchell's St. John's-wort (*H. mitchellianum*), is less common than Mountain St. John's-wort. It grows in the same habitats but has many more flowers in each cluster (up to 60). The protruding stamens of Mountain St. John's-wort can be up to ¼" long.

This plant and *H. mitchellianum* are southern Appalachian endemics and are known to hybridize when they occur together.

◆ **HABITAT**—Seeps, grassy balds, and grassy openings.
◆ **LOCATIONS**—Clingmans Dome Road, The Boulevard Trail.
◆ **BLOOMS JULY - SEPTEMBER**

# YELLOW STAR GRASS

*Hypoxis hirsuta*

Lily Family
*(Liliaceae)*

Plant: 2"-8"
(5-20 cm)
Flower: ½"-¾"
(1-2 cm)

Low-mid elevation
Common

Jessie M. Harris

It would be easy to miss this delicate little herb with long narrow leaves like grass. But look for the constellations of bright yellow, six-pointed stars rising from inside a clump of the basal leaves and you will be rewarded with their delicate beauty. One to three flowers are borne upon each slender stalk, and each stalk is whiskered with fine hairs. The undersides of the three petals and the three identical sepals are not only hairy, but green, in contrast to the yellow color of the open flower. When not in flower, this member of the Lily family could be easily confused with the true grasses.

All this hairiness must have impressed the person who named this low-growing species, as he called it *hirsuta*, Latin for hairy.

◆ **HABITAT**—Woodlands.

◆ **LOCATIONS**—Rich Mountain Road, Noland Divide Trail.

◆ BLOOMS APRIL - JUNE

*Hypericum mutilum*

St. John's-wort Family
*(Clusiaceae)*

Plant: 4"-30"
(1-8 dm)
Flower: ¹⁄₁₆"
(3-4 mm)

Wide range
Frequent

Jessie M. Harris

Unlike its more famous plant cousins, *Hypericum perforatum* and *H. punctatum*, Dwarf St. John's-wort is not used to treat depression. The main stem branches many times above the middle of the plant. The leaves are elliptic or oval, smooth-edged, opposite and clasping the stem. The flowers have 5 sepals, 5 petals, and numerous (5-22) stamens. The petals and sepals have translucent dots, but no black dots or streaks. A single plant usually has many tiny yellow flowers. There are nine different species of St. John's-wort in the park. Because many of them bloom near the Summer Solstice (June 21) and the Feast of St. John the Baptist (June 24), people attributed wondrous powers to the plants. If you need to repel lightning, ward off the evil eye, or reveal the identity of a witch, St. John's-wort is the plant for you!

◆ **HABITAT**—Bogs, marshes, wet soils.
◆ BLOOMS JUNE - OCTOBER

# WHORLED LOOSESTRIFE

Jessie M. Harris

*Lysimachia
quadrifolia*

Primrose Family
(*Primulaceae*)

Plant: 1'-3'
(3-10 dm)
Flower: ½"
(1.5 cm)

Low-mid elevation
Frequent

"Whorled" and "*quadrifolia*" (four leaves) accurately describe this native perennial wildflower. The sessile or short-stalked leaves are found in whorls of 4 (rarely 3 to 6). The largest leaves (3" long, 1" wide) are found in the middle of the stout, unbranched stem. Delicate solitary yellow flowers on long stalks (1-2 inches) grow in whorls from the upper 2-6 whorls of leaves. The five petals and five sepals are streaked with black. The genus is named for Lyimachus, companion of Alexander the Great and King of Thrace (361-281 B.C.E.) who, in desperation, seized a bunch of flowers to pacify a bull that was chasing him. Whorled loosestrife is not related to purple loosestrife (*Lythrum salicaria L.*), an invasive non-native.

◆ **HABITAT**—Wet or dry soil in thin woods or full sun.
◆ **LOCATION**—Cades Cove woods edges.
◆ BLOOMS MAY - AUGUST

Buttercup Family
(*Ranunculaceae*)

Plant: 6"-30"
(15-76 cm)
Flower: ¾"
(1.9 cm)

Wide range
Common

Jessie M. Harris

The specific name, *hispidus*, can be translated from the Latin to mean bristly. This is an excellent description of the tall stems of this plant. Each of the alternate leaves is deeply divided into three parts. These may be further lobed.

The yellow petals (usually five) encircle a flower head packed with numerous pistils and stamens. The petals and the five green, spreading sepals make this the showiest buttercup included in this book. Sometimes this and other buttercups are mistaken for cinquefoils or even wild strawberries, but buttercups have more pistils and stamens than the others. Scientists theorize that similar-looking species develop to take advantage of similar pollinators.

◆ **HABITAT**—Dry woods and meadows.

◆ **LOCATIONS**—Rich Mtn. Road, Lower Mount Cammerer Tr.

◆ BLOOMS MARCH - JUNE

# SMALL-FLOWERED BUTTERCUP

Jessie M. Harris

*Ranunculus abortivus*

Buttercup Family
(*Ranunculaceae*)

Plant: 6"-20"
(15-51 cm)
Flower: ¼"
(0.6 cm)

Low-mid elevation
Common

This is also called kidney-leaved buttercup for its rosette of kidney-shaped basal leaves. Along the stem the leaves are most often divided into three parts, sometimes appearing to be separate leaves. Solitary flowers composed of five recurved sepals and five yellow petals arise from the axils of these leaves. Like other buttercups, the flowers are characterized by numerous stamens and pistils.

There are 13 species of buttercups (nine native and four introduced) in the park; specific identification is very technical. Of the buttercups discussed in this book, this is the shortest and the only one without a hairy stem. Buttercups tend to produce very little nectar. They reward their pollinators instead with nutritious pollen.

◆ **HABITAT**— Fields, woods, thickets, and roadsides.

◆ **LOCATIONS**—Greenbrier Road, Lower Mount Cammerer Trail.

◆ BLOOMS MARCH - JUNE

## Trillium luteum

# YELLOW TRILLIUM

Lily Family
*(Liliaceae)*

Plant: 6"-12"
(15-30 cm)
Flower: 1"-2"
(2.5-5 cm)

Low elevation
Frequent

Ed Pomikwia

This attractive trillium has a single, yellow, lemon-scented flower. The petals are narrow and erect, giving it a "closed" appearance. Its leaves exhibit a camouflage-like mottling. A similar species, sessile-flowered maroon trillium (*T. cuneatum*), is only occasionally seen at low elevations. Its ill-scented flowers are larger and a reddish-brown to maroon color, while still manifesting the erect closed appearance. *T. cuneatum's* leaves are also mottled.

Trillium is derived from the Latin prefix "tri," meaning three. All trilliums are characterized by having their parts in threes or multiples thereof. They have three leaves, three petals, three sepals, three stigmas, and six stamens. Even the berries have three or six sides.

◆ **HABITAT**—Moist woods.
◆ **LOCATIONS**—Tremont Road, Cove Hardwood Nature Trail.
◆ **BLOOMS APRIL - MAY**

161

# SUNDROPS

*Oenothera fruticosa*

Evening Primrose
Family
*(Onagraceae)*

Plant: 12"-36"
(30-92 cm)
Flower: 1"-2"
(2.5-5 cm)

Low-mid elevation
Occasional

Bill Lea

Sundrop blossoms are bright yellow with a prominent cross-shaped stigma in the center. The eight pollen-producing stamens are clearly visible as well. Its four large petals are veiny and conspicuously notched. The lance-shaped leaves are toothed and alternate. Often the leaves have reddish-purple spots. The seed pods are about twice as long as wide.

This plant's flowers are open during the day and closed at night. Evening primroses, relatives of sundrops, are closed in daylight and open at twilight. The park has a variety of animals that pollinate plants. Bees, flies, butterflies, wasps, and birds are active during the day. Moths and beetles are nocturnal pollinators.

◆ **HABITAT**—Dry open woods, meadows, and roadsides.

◆ **LOCATIONS**—Balsam Mountain Road, Anthony Creek Trail.

◆ BLOOMS APRIL - AUGUST

*Rugelia nudicaulis*

# RUGEL'S RAGWORT

Aster Family
(*Asteraceae*)

Plant: 12″-20″
(30-50 cm)
Flower head: ½″
**wide** (1 cm)

High elevation
Occasional

*leaf*

Ken Voorhis

This plant may not win any beauty contests, but it is amazing nonetheless. It is found only in Great Smoky Mountains National Park. Ironically, it is abundant along some high elevation trails here. There are usually several nodding flower heads per plant. Long, pointed bracts surround the blossom forming an urn from which the yellow or straw-colored disk flowers protrude. The stem bearing the flowers has a few small stalkless leaves. Most of the leaves are heart-shaped and have large teeth and long stems.

As non-native insects kill the Fraser fir trees in the park, more sunlight reaches and dries the forest floor. Park botanists do not yet know what effect these changes will have on Rugel's ragwort.

◆ **HABITAT**—High elevation moist hardwood and spruce-fir forests.
◆ **LOCATIONS**—Clingmans Dome Road, The Boulevard Trail.
◆ BLOOMS JUNE - AUGUST

# Rattlesnake Hawkweed

Harry Ellis

*Hieracium venosum*

Aster Family
(*Asteraceae*)

Plant: 8″-24″
(20-61 cm)
Flower heads: ½″-
¾″
(1.3-1.9 cm)

Low-mid elevation
Common

Rattlesnake hawkweed has dandelion-like flower heads. Unlike dandelion, however, it is native to North America and common in woodlands. There can be several flower heads on each plant. The petals are golden yellow and each is fringed at the tip. The leaves are striking: oval, densely hairy, and purple-veined.

Several wildflowers in the Smoky Mountains have "snake" or "rattlesnake" as a common name. Sometimes the plant was used to treat snakebite. In the case of rattlesnake hawkweed, the name comes from the network of purple veins on the leaves, a "snake skin" pattern. "*Hieracium*" comes from "*hierax*" or "hawk." Ancient Greeks thought that hawks ate the plant to improve their eyesight.

- **HABITAT**—Open, dry woodlands and forest edges.
- **LOCATIONS**—Cades Cove Loop Road, Chestnut Top Trail.
- BLOOMS APRIL - JULY

# MARYLAND GOLDEN ASTER

*Chrysopsis mariana*

Aster Family
(*Asteraceae*)

Plant: 12"-30"
(30-77 cm)
Flower head: ½"-1"
(1.3-2.5 cm)

Low-mid elevation
Frequent

Harry Ellis

This knee-high plant has daisy-like flower heads with yellow ray and disk flowers. The ray flowers (outer petals) are widest in the middle, then taper to the tip. The leaves are untoothed or sometimes very obscurely toothed, arranged alternately on the stem, and oblong. Similar looking grass-leaved golden aster (*Pityopsis graminifolia*), also found frequently in the park, has silvery, silky, grass-like leaves.

A common method of preventing self-pollination in members of the aster family is for the pollen-receiving organ (pistil) and pollen-producing organs (anthers) to mature at slightly different times. Hence, when plant "A" has only flowers with mature pistils, it relies on its neighbor, plant "B," to have only ripe anthers.

◆ **HABITAT**—Rocky, dry woods and openings.
◆ **LOCATIONS**—Cades Cove Loop Road, Cooper Road Trail.
◆ BLOOMS JUNE - OCTOBER

# Mountain Krigia

*Krigia montana*

Aster Family
(*Asteraceae*)

Plant: 4"-16"
(10-41 cm)
Flower head: ½"-1"
(1.3-2.5 cm)

High elevation
Scarce

Ken Voorhis

If you are walking one of the trails near the top of Mt. Le Conte and
see a dandelion, look closer, you may have found a rare plant. The ray
flowers are bright yellow-orange, have fringed tips, and are each about
½" long. The bracts at the base of the flower head are leafy and green
(sometimes with a darker tip) and about half the length of the rays.
Flowering heads are solitary on the stem, but there may be several
flowering stems in a clump of plants. Most of the leaves are basal,
though there may be a few on the flowering stem. The leaves are variable: some linear, some lance-shaped, and some very lobed, toothed,
and dandelion-like. There are three other Krigia in the park, but all
favor lower elevations and are not southern Appalachian endemics.

◆ **HABITAT**—Crevices of moist cliffs, grassy balds, Mt. Le Conte.
◆ **LOCATIONS**—The Boulevard Trail, Alum Cave Trail.
◆ **BLOOMS JUNE - SEPTEMBER**

*Coreopsis major*

Aster Family
(*Asteraceae*)

Plant: 18"-36"
(46-92 cm)
Flower head:
1"-2½"
(2.5-6 cm)

Low-mid elevation
Common

*leaves*

Ken Voorhis

Wood tickseed has seven or more bright yellow ray flowers (outer petals) surrounding red or yellow disk flowers. The tips of the ray flowers are generally not notched. The leaves are divided into three leaflets with edges that are untoothed, though they may be slightly wavy. The three-pointed leaves are stalkless and opposite so superficially the plant appears to have six leaves in a whorl around the stem. Hairy tickseed (*C. pubescens*) is hairy throughout and has notched rays; coreopsis (*C. tinctoria*) has notched rays, linear leaves, is non-native and has been found only in low elevation dry fields.

Don't worry—ticks don't live on this plant. Both the common and scientific names refer to the tick-like shape of the seed.

◆ **HABITAT**—Dry, open woods.
◆ **LOCATIONS**—Balsam Mountain Road, Gregory Ridge Trail.
◆ BLOOMS JUNE - AUGUST

# THREE-LOBED BLACK-EYED SUSAN

Joseph G. Strauch, Jr.

*Rudbeckia triloba*

Aster Family
(Asteraceae)

Plant: 3'-5'
(1-1.6 m)
Flower head:
2½"-4"
(6-10 cm)

Wide range
Common

This wildflower is a short-lived perennial. The stem is branched and somewhat hairy. Although the leaves are variable in size and shape, the lower leaves are generally lobed or divided. The number of flower heads on an individual plant is also variable. The bracts surrounding the base of each flower head are narrow, green, and leafy. Each head has 6-12 yellow or orange ray flowers (outer petals) ½"-1" long. The disk is less than ½" across and composed of dark purple flowers.

   *R. triloba* is the only park species with lobed and divided lower leaves. *R. hirta* is a prairie plant that has moved eastward with human disturbance. It is coarsely hairy and is found only in open areas. *R. fulgida* is smooth or has short hairs and is found in dry woods.

+ **HABITAT**—Woodlands and moist areas.
+ **LOCATIONS**—Cades Cove Loop Road, Noland Divide Trail.
+ **BLOOMS JULY - OCTOBER**

Aster Family
(*Asteraceae*)

Plant: 3'-5'
(0.9-1.5 m)
Flower head: 2½"-
4" (6-10 cm)

Wide Range
Common

Jessie M. Harris

Coneflower is a perennial with a stout base. The leaves are large, stalked, and the lower ones are deeply lobed into 3-7 irregular leaflets. The flower heads have 6-16 yellow rays (1"-2½" long) that droop beneath the disk. This is the only coneflower in the park that has greenish-yellow disk flowers. The disk is thimble-shaped, and is ½"-1" in diameter. Orange coneflowers (*R. fulgida, R. umbrosa, R. triloba,* and *R. hirta*) are found at low elevations. They have orange ray flowers and purple or brown disk flowers and are popularly known as black-eyed Susans.

Because coneflower is often found along shady mountain streams, it is one of the most characteristic species of the park.

◆ **HABITAT**—Wet woods and thickets.
◆ **LOCATIONS**—Balsam Mountain Road, Clingmans Dome Trail.
◆ BLOOMS JULY ‑ OCTOBER

# WIDE-LEAVED SUNFLOWER

Harry Ellis

*Helianthus decapetalus*

Aster Family
(*Asteraceae*)

Plant: 2'-5'
(0.6-1.5 m)
Flower head:
1½"-4"
(3.8-10 cm)

Wide range
Frequent

This is one of seven species of sunflowers in the park. Wide-leaved sunflower has several flower heads on a single plant. The 8-15 ray flowers (outer petals) are yellow, and ½"-1½" long. The disk is yellow and ½"-¾" across. The stem is hairy in the flower cluster, but smooth elsewhere. Leaves are opposite on the stem, and the lower ones have long stalks. All are toothed and rough in texture. Look on the underside of the leaf for a pair of prominent veins running parallel to the midrib.

Wide-leaved sunflower is related to common sunflower (*H. annuus*), grown for seed and oil. Songbirds relish the high energy oils found in sunflower seeds.

◆ **HABITAT**—Dry woods.

◆ **LOCATIONS**—Balsam Mountain Road, Gregory Bald Trail.

◆ **BLOOMS JULY - OCTOBER**

# MOUNTAIN BELLWORT

Lily Family
*(Liliaceae)*

Plant: 6"-12"
(15-30 cm)
Flower: 1"
(2.5 cm)

Low-mid elevation
Frequent

Jessie M. Harris

Bellworts have solitary, yellow, hanging flowers that are often partially hidden by leaves. In mountain bellwort and wild oats (*U. sessilfolia*) the leaves are not clasping of the stem (see large-flowered bellwort). With mountain bellwort the leaves are shiny and the stems are clumped. The leaves of wild oats are dull and the stems are more sparsely distributed.

Many Smokies' wildflowers, especially those of the cool high elevations, have ranges that stretch far to the north. Mountain bellwort, however, can be found only in the Southeast. Its common name comes from its hanging, bell-like flower. Wort comes from Old English and means simply plant. Bellwort seeds are dispersed by ants.

◆ **HABITAT**—Dry to moist woods.
◆ **LOCATION**—Noland Divide Trail.
◆ BLOOMS APRIL - MAY

# Large-flowered Bellwort

Joseph G. Strauch, Jr.

*Uvularia grandiflora*

Lily Family
(*Liliaceae*)

Plant: 12"-24"
(30-61 cm)
Flower: 1½"
(3.8 cm)

Low-mid elevation
Frequent

This plant's sunny yellow flowers dangle beneath the upper leaves of its slender, arching stem. The long, narrow, look-alike sepals and petals (three each) together form a constricted bell-shaped flower. The base of the narrowly oval, alternate leaves is so clasping of the stem that it appears to be growing right through the leaves.

While this species tends to be encountered in dense clumps, a similar species, perfoliate bellwort (*U. perfoliata*) is usually found in sparser colonies. It is a scaled-down version, with a shorter stem and smaller flowers. While the large-flowered bellwort is smooth inside the blossom, the inner surface of the perfoliate bellwort is covered with tiny glands which create a rough texture.

◆ **HABITAT**—Rich, moist woods.

◆ **LOCATIONS**—Rich Mountain Road, Kanati Fork Trail.

◆ BLOOMS  APRIL - MAY

## *Thalictrum dioicum*

# EARLY MEADOWRUE

Buttercup Family
(*Ranunculaceae*)

Plant: 6″-24″
(15-61 cm)
Flower: to ¼″ wide
(0.6 cm)

Low-mid elevation
Frequent

Jessie M. Harris

Early meadowrue leaves are unusual in that they are thrice compound. The many leaflets are further divided into 3-9 rounded lobes, giving the plant a very bushy appearance.

Even more unusual are the plant's flowers. As the name, *dioicum* (two-households) implies, there are separate male and female plants, each with the appropriate flowers. The female flowers are composed of 3-8 tiny purplish pistils. Since neither flower has petals and only very small sepals, the female flowers often go unnoticed. The male flowers, with their numerous, dangling, yellow anthers, bear a resemblance to Chinese lanterns.

Native Americans used meadowrue as a treatment for deafness.

◆ **HABITAT**—Rich woods.
◆ **LOCATIONS**—Lower Mount Cammerer Tr., Rich Mountain Rd.
◆ BLOOMS MARCH - APRIL

# YELLOW MANDARIN     *Disporum lanuginosum*

Lily Family
*(Liliaceae)*

Plant: 8"-24"
(20-61 cm)
Flower: 1"
(2.5 cm)

Low-mid elevation
Common

Rob Simpson

Yellow mandarin flowers have slender, yellowish-green sepals and petals which resemble dangling tentacles. It superficially resembles false Solomon's seal, but yellow mandarin has several branches. The 2"-4" leaves have well-defined parallel veins. Consider yourself lucky if you encounter the other species of this genus in the park, the spotted mandarin (*D. maculatum*). Scarce, but striking, it has creamy white flowers with green and purple speckles.

Both mandarins resemble the bellworts (*Uvularia spp.*) and twisted stalk (*Streptopus spp.*), which is also sometimes referred to as mandarin. However, the sepals and petals of the mandarins remain straight, while those of twisted stalk turn up.

◆ **HABITAT**—Moist woods, coves.

◆ **LOCATIONS**—Balsam Mtn. Road, Cove Hardwood Nature Trail.

◆ BLOOMS APRIL - MAY

# YELLOW LADY'S SLIPPER

*Cypripedium pubescens*

Orchid Family
(*Orchidaceae*)

Plant: 12"-24"
(30-61 cm)
Flower: Variable in
size, pouch-like lip
petal usually
¾"-2.5"
(1.9-6 cm)

Low-mid elevation
Occasional

Jessie M. Harris

This native orchid is a delight to find. Look closely and discover it differs from pink lady's slipper not only in flower color, but also in the presence of 3-5 leaves on the flower stalk. The flowering stalk usually has 1-2 blossoms at the top. The blossom's lateral petals are greenish-yellow to purplish-brown and delicately twisted. The lip or pouch is bright yellow with purple veins.

Individual orchids produce thousands of seeds, but they must find the right fungi in the soil to survive.

Lady's slippers are particular favorites of wildflower photographers. Please take care when photographing any plant not to damage it or the plants around it. Careful placement of feet (yours and the tripod's) is essential!

◆ **HABITAT**—Dry to moist woods.
◆ BLOOMS APRIL - JUNE

# PALE JEWELWEED

*Impatiens pallida*

Touch-me-not
Family
(*Balsaminaceae*)

Plant: 2′-4′
(.6-1.2 m)
Flower:1″
(2.5 cm)

Wide range
Common

Ken Voorhis

This has very similar flowers to the orange jewelweed (*I. capensis*). Its yellow coloration and side-turned sepal spur will differentiate the two. Both plants are also called snapweed and touch-me-not, because of their fruit. The seeds mature inside a tightly coiled capsule. When ripe, the capsule "explodes" if touched, dispersing the seed. Carefully enclose a ripe fruit in your hands and capture its contents. Remove the coiled attachment to expose the robin-egg blue seed inside. This edible seed tastes like a sunflower seed.

Many people maintain the sap of this plant will ease poison ivy itch. A rare, cream-colored version of pale jewelweed occurs on cold, north-facing slopes at high elevations.

◆ **HABITAT**—Moist woods, light gaps, coves.
◆ **LOCATIONS**—Newfound Gap Road, Little River Trail.
◆ **BLOOMS JUNE - SEPTEMBER**

*Conopholis americana*

Broomrape Family
(*Orobanchaceae*)

Plant: 4"-10"
(10-25 cm)
Flower: ½"
(1 cm)

Low-mid elevation
Frequent

Bill Lea

Looking like a small ear of corn peeking up through the leaf litter, this plant is a remarkable find. Look closely to see the tiny yellowish-brown flowers. The gently curving upper petals are fused into two lobes; the lower lip is composed of three fused petals. This lip is shorter, allowing the four stamens to protrude from the flower. Each of the numerous flowers is protected by a bract.

There are no leaves here or even chlorophyll; the plant doesn't need them. Squawroot is a parasite. Its roots penetrate those of oak trees and draw food. Some call it cancer-root because of this habit.

Black bears in the Smoky Mountains are known to feed on this plant.

◆ **HABITAT**—Dry oak woods.
◆ **LOCATIONS**—Rich Mountain Road, Chestnut Top Trail.
◆ BLOOMS APRIL - AUGUST

# WOOD BETONY

*Pedicularis canadensis*

Snapdragon Family
(*Scrophulariaceae*)

Plant: 8″-12″
(20-30 cm)
Flower: ¾″
(1.9 cm)

Wide range
Common

Harry Ellis

Clustered together at the apex of a thick, hairy stem are divided leaves and colorful flowers. The alternate leaves are so finely cut that they are often mistaken for ferns. The flowers are surprisingly beautiful. Each bloom is composed of two lips. The upper red lip is divided into two lobes which curve above the lower, three-toothed, yellow lip. These form a tight tube housing the reproductive organs.

Some believe that because of a relationship with a fungus, this plant will not grow well outside its natural habitat. Folklore has saddled this beautiful blossom with an ugly name, lousewort. Farmers erroneously thought it causes lice in their cattle. Even the genus, *Pedicularis*, means "of the lice."

◆ **HABITAT**—Open woods.

◆ **LOCATIONS**—Rich Mountain Road, Porters Creek Trail.

◆ BLOOMS APRIL - JUNE

Parsley Family
(*Apiaceae*)

Plant: 2'-4'
(0.6-1.2 m)
Flower: minute
flowers in clusters
2"-6" wide
(4-15 cm)

High elevation
Common

Jessie M. Harris

This robust wildflower is hard to miss, even when not in bloom. Many people comment on its stout, vigorous appearance as it first emerges from the ground. The individual flowers are minute and greenish-yellow in color. Angelica's leaves are compound with coarsely toothed leaflets. Hairy angelica (*A. venenosa*) is also found in the park, but at low to middle elevation and at drier sites.

Most plants in the parsley family produce scented oils which make some of them important culinary herbs (e.g., fennel, dill). However, several species (including several angelicas) are dangerously poisonous. Bees apparently become intoxicated after feeding on angelica flowers and have been observed behaving crazily.

♦ **HABITAT**—Open rocky woods, meadows, and stream banks.
♦ **LOCATIONS**—Balsam Mountain Road, The Boulevard Trail.
♦ BLOOMS AUGUST - SEPTEMBER

# MEADOW-PARSNIP

*Thaspium barbinode*

Parsley Family
(*Apiaceae*)

Plant: 1-4 feet
(30-120 cm)
Flower: cluster 1"-
2½" across
(2.5-6 cm)

Low-mid elevation
Frequent

Harry Ellis

*umbel*

Meadow-parsnip has minute yellow flowers in a broad, branched cluster. Look closely and note that the central flower of each cluster is on a tiny stalk. The stalk may be easier to see in a cluster that has already gone to seed. The leaves are divided into leaflets. Note the stiff hairs at the base of each leaf where it joins the stem. Yellow and purple meadow-parsnip (*T. trifoliatum* var. *aureum* or var. *trifoliatum*, respectively) are not hairy at the nodes. The central flower (and seed) of similar-looking golden Alexanders (*Zizia* spp.) is not stalked.

The way flowers are arranged on a plant is termed "inflorescence." Learn to recognize the "umbel" or umbrella-like design of meadow parsnip and you have learned to recognize the Parsley family.

◆ **HABITAT**—Woods, stream banks.
◆ **LOCATION**—Noland Divide Trail, Balsam Mountain Road.
◆ BLOOMS  APRIL - MAY

*Solidago canadensis var. scabra*

Aster Family (Asteraceae)

Plant: 1′-5′ (.3-1.6 m)
Flower heads: ¼″ (.6 cm)

Wide range
Frequent

Jessie M. Harris

There are 19 species of goldenrods in the park. Canada goldenrod, one of the most common species, is a tall perennial from a creeping underground root. The main stem is usually smooth near the base and downy upward. The leaves are lance-shaped, toothed, three-veined, stalkless, and rough. The flower cluster is at the top of the plant and consists of many long arching branches. Each head consists of 7-17 minute ray flowers (outer petals) and fewer disk flowers.

Say "goldenrod" and people immediately think of runny noses and sneezing. This is actually inaccurate. Goldenrod blossoms are insect pollinated, so little of their pollen becomes air-borne. Ragweed (*Ambrosia* spp) is more commonly the cause of hayfever misery.

◆ **HABITAT**—Thickets, clearings, and meadows.
◆ **LOCATIONS**—Newfound Gap Road, Schoolhouse Gap Trail.
◆ BLOOMS JULY - OCTOBER

# YELLOW RAGWORT

*Senecio anonymus*

Aster Family
(*Asteraceae*)

Plant: 1-2'
(.3-.6 m)
Flower head:
¼"wide
(.6 cm)

Low-mid elevation
Common

Harry Ellis

Yellow ragwort has numerous (20-100) daisy-like flower heads. Both the ray flowers (outer petals) and disk flowers are yellow. The plant can have several stems, and these are woolly at the base of the plant. The basal leaves are elliptical with long leafy stalks and are toothed or wavy-edged. The stem leaves are feathery and become increasingly stalkless and smaller toward the top of the plant.

Golden ragwort (*S. aureus*) has basal leaves with heart-shaped bases and long thin stalks. Spatulate-leaved ragwort (*S. obovatus*) has spoon-shaped leaves.

The white fluff on the mature seeds of yellow ragwort resemble an old man's white beard. *Senecio* means "old man" in Latin.

◆ **HABITAT**—Meadows and dry woods.
◆ **LOCATIONS**—Cades Cove Loop Road, Schoolhouse Gap Trail.
◆ BLOOMS MAY - JUNE

Mint Family
*(Lamiaceae)*

Plant: 2'-3'
(0.6-0.9 m)
Flower: ½″ two
protruding stamens
(1.3 cm)

Low-mid elevation
Frequent

Jessie M. Harris

This tall plant has small, delicate, light yellow flowers in loose, branching clusters. The lower lip of each flower is conspicuously fringed. Two stamens protrude from each side of the flower. At flowering time, stoneroot can be almost waist high. Like many mints, it has a square stem. Large, coarsely toothed leaves are paired along the stem. All parts of this plant are fragrant: the flowers are delicately lemon-scented and the foliage is reminiscent of citronella.

The large, knobby, stone-like root of this plant was used by both Native Americans and European settlers to treat urinary ailments of man and beast. An alternate common name, "richweed," comes from the rich soils it prefers.

◆ **HABITAT**—Rich, moist woods.
◆ **LOCATIONS**—Balsam Mountain Road, Bote Mountain Trail.
◆ BLOOMS AUGUST - OCTOBER

# Skunk Goldenrod

*Solidago glomerata*

Aster Family
(*Asteraceae*)

Plant: 6"-24"
(15-60 cm)
Flower head: ½"-¾"
(1-2 cm)

High elevation
Frequent

Bill Lea

Use your nose to identify this plant. If you are at the higher elevations (above 4,500') and smell skunk, look around for skunk goldenrod. The flower clusters are not on nodding, arched branches like many goldenrods. Rather, the clusters are in a spike at the top of the stem. Each head is large, coarse, and composed of about eight ray flowers (outer petals) and 13-34 disk flowers.

It is curious that this plant's skunk smell cannot be detected from the crushed foliage or flowers, but simply forms a cloud around the plants. Skunk goldenrod is endemic to the southern Appalachians. In fact, the only place in the world it is found is in 13 counties of North Carolina and Tennessee.

◆ **HABITAT**—Grassy balds, spruce-fir forests, and rocky outcrops.
◆ **LOCATIONS**—Balsam Mountain Road, Clingmans Dome Trail.
◆ BLOOMS AUGUST - OCTOBER

*Viola pedata*

# BIRD'S FOOT VIOLET

Violet Family
(*Violaceae*)

Plant: 4"-10"
(10-25 cm)
Flower: 1"-1½"
(2.5-3.8 cm)

Low-mid elevation
Occasional

Bill Lea

While most violets have heart-shaped leaves, the bird's foot violet has thrice-divided leaves which somewhat resemble a bird's foot. The flowers of the bird's foot violet are held high above the leaves and sometimes as many as 30 flowers are produced in one season. The five lilac-colored petals of each flower are arranged in the same plane giving the flowers a flat, two-dimensional appearance (a characteristic that separates this plant from all other Smokies' violets). The bright orange anthers protrude noticeably beyond the petals.

This violet is larger than most and is known to be pollinated by bees and butterflies. Sometimes smaller and shorter flowers are produced in the summer and autumn.

◆ **HABITAT**—Dry, rocky woods.
◆ **LOCATIONS**—Rich Mountain Road, Cooper Road Trail.
◆ **BLOOMS MARCH - MAY**

# WOOLLY BLUE VIOLET

*Viola sororia*

Violet Family
(*Violaceae*)

Plant: 4"-10"
(10-25 cm)
Flower: ½"-1"
(1.3-2.5 cm)

Low-mid elevation
Common

Jessie M. Harris

The woolly blue is a large-flowered violet. As the common name suggests, it is indeed woolly or hairy unless found growing in open sunny places. The leaf stems of the woolly blue violet are characteristically thick and fleshy. Its flower stalks do not bear leaves—hence, this is a member of the "stemless" group of violet.

The woolly blue violet resembles the marsh blue violet (*V. cucullata*); both have similar flowers, but the latter's has a dark center. Although the two species grow within the same elevation range, the marsh blue violet is usually found in moister habitats, such as streamsides and marshes. Variable in appearance and habitats, this is our most adaptable violet.

- ◆ **HABITAT**—Moist to dry woods, trailsides.
- ◆ **LOCATION**—Big Creek Trail.
- ◆ **BLOOMS MARCH - APRIL**

*Hydrophyllum virginianum*

Waterleaf Family
*(Hydrophyllaceae)*

Plant: 8"-30"
(2-7 dm)
Flower: Less than ½"
(1 cm)
Flower cluster:
1¼"-2" across
(3-5 cm)

Mid-high elevation
Occasional

Jessie M. Harris

There are three waterleaf species in the park, and they differ in elevation range and in abundance within the Great Smokies. The easiest way to distinguish them is by examining their leaves. Both stem and basal leaves of Virginia waterleaf are pinnately lobed, and each lobe has sharp serrate edges. The basal leaves of Canadian waterleaf (*H. canadense*) are pinnately lobed, whereas the leaves toward the top of the plant are palmately lobed and resemble maple leaves. Bigleaf waterleaf (*H. macrophyllum*) also has pinnately lobed leaves, but each leaf is larger, and the serrations are more rounded, than those of Virginia waterleaf. The leaves of all three species have white mottling that may look like drops of water. All species have white to lavender flowers.

◆ **HABITAT**—Cove forests, rocky stream banks, and rich forests.
◆ **LOCATION**—Cataloochee Divide Trail.
◆ **BLOOMS APRIL - JUNE**

# BEAKED VIOLET

*Viola rostrata*

Violet Family
(*Violaceae*)

Plant: 4"-8"
(10-20 cm)
Flower: ½"-¾"
(1.3-1.9- cm)

Low-mid elevation
Occasional

Jessie M. Harris

*spurred petal*

$\mathrm{T}$he beaked violet was named for the slender upward curving protrusion on the flower's lower (spurred) petal. All violets have a spurred petal, but this flower's spur measures ½"-1" long, making it easy to distinguish from the others. The flower of the beaked violet is a pale shade of violet that is different from the deeper purples of other violets in the Great Smokies. The lower three petals have dark blue lines, or nectar guides. This species is a "stemmed violet," so named because it has leaves that alternate along an above ground stem (rather than a circular cluster of leaves on a leaf stem).

The flower size and shade of purple-blue may vary from plant to plant or between populations.

• **HABITAT**—Moist, rich woods, often near Eastern hemlock trees.
• **LOCATIONS**—Greenbrier Road, Bradley Fork Trail.
• **BLOOMS APRIL - MAY**

# *Gentiana decora*

# MOUNTAIN GENTIAN

Gentian Family
(*Gentianaceae*)

Plant: 12″-24″
(30-61 cm)
Flower: 1″-2″
(2.5-5 cm)

Low-mid elevation
Frequent

Hugh Nourse

When the first trees turn red in September, this gentian begins to brighten the forest. Three to 12 pale blue to violet blossoms form a compact cluster atop the stems of this plant. The five-lobed, tubular corolla is striped with blue or violet to guide insects. It maintains its "closed" appearance throughout the blooming period.

A thin pleat connects each of the tiny petal lobes. This delicately fringed tissue may be from half as long to slightly longer than the lobes. It may serve to protect the flower from crawling insects by failing under their weight. Hence, only flying insects can successfully enter the tight flower to act as pollinators.

This is the most common gentian in the park.

◆ **HABITAT**—Wooded slopes, stream banks, dry woods, trailsides.
◆ **LOCATIONS**—Rich Mountain Road, Rainbow Falls Trail.
◆ **BLOOMS SEPTEMBER - OCTOBER**

# BLUE PHLOX

*Phlox divaricata*

Phlox Family
(*Polemoniaceae*)

Plant: 10"-20"
(25-51)
Flower: 1"
(2.5 cm)

Low-mid elevation
Occasional

Ed Pomikwia

*tube with
anthers*

This tall spring plant is topped with a dazzling display of blue to purple flowers. The five notched petals radiate from a very narrow tube. Look for a closed flower bud. These tightly wrapped buds spiral like a torch. Some attribute this characteristic for the name phlox which is Greek for flame.

Nine native and two exotic phloxes have been found in the park. Seven of the native species are occasionally encountered. Creeping phlox (*P. stolonifera*) has creeping stems that form loose mats. Broad-leaved (*P. amplifolia*) and summer phlox (*P. paniculata*) have leaves with prominent side veins. Blue phlox is the only species with a loose cluster of flowers and a style shorter than the lowest anthers.

◆ **HABITAT**—Rich Woods.
◆ **LOCATIONS**—Newfound Gap Road, Porters Creek Trail.
◆ **BLOOMS APRIL - JUNE**

## CRESTED DWARF IRIS

*Iris cristata*

Iris Family
(*Iridaceae*)

Plant: 4"-9"
(10-23 cm)
Flower: 2½"
(6 cm)

Low-mid elevation
Common

Bill Lea

This complex flower has three blue-purple (rarely albino) petals as a standard above three unique petal-like sepals. On each sepal is a yellow crest which leads pollinating insects toward the nectar hidden deep in the flower. The insect pollinators first pass beneath the stigmas (depositing pollen) then the anthers (receiving new pollen) before exiting this one-way flower near the stem. This elaborate system assures cross-pollination.

The similar spring dwarf iris (*I. verna*) has narrower leaves (less than ½" wide) and lacks the crest on the sepals. Some say it has a stronger fragrance than the crested dwarf iris. Spring dwarf iris is less common and prefers dry pine forests.

◆ **HABITAT**—Rich, moist open woods, trailsides.
◆ **LOCATIONS**—Roaring Fork Motor Nature Tr., Bradley Fork Tr.
◆ **BLOOMS APRIL - MAY**

# WILLOW AMSONIA

*Amsonia tabernaemontana*

Dogbane Family
(*Apocynaceae*)

Plant: 1'-2'
(3-7 dm)
Flower: ½"-1"
(12-25 mm)

Low
Rare

Jessie M. Harris

W illow amsonia is a perennial that usually has two or three unbranched, smooth stems arising from a woody rootstock. Leaves are thin in texture, are arranged alternately up the stem, and are 3"-6" (5-15 cm) long. The flowers are grouped at the top of each main stem, and each flower has a minute stalk (pedicel). It is prudent to approach plants in the Dogbane family with caution: chemicals in the juice range from mildly irritating (willow amsonia), to potent medicinals (anti-tumor alkyloids in *Catharanthus*, the Madagascar-periwinkle), to deadly toxic (ornamental Oleander, *Nerium*). Mourning cloak butterflies and other insects active in early spring gather nectar from the sky blue flowers.

♦ **HABITAT**—Moist forests, low woods, streambanks.
♦ **LOCATION**—Chilhowee cliffs.
♦ **BLOOMS APRIL**

# BLUE-EYED GRASS

*Sisyrinchium
angustifolium*

Iris Family
(*Iridaceae*)

Plant: 4"-20"
(10-51 cm)
Flower: ½"
(1.3 cm)

Wide ranging
Frequent

Tom Barnes

With long, thin, grass-like leaves, this tiniest of the irises is overlooked unless in bloom. The pale to deep blue flowers sit atop flattened stems. Six dark-lined sepals and petals radiate from a central yellow spot. These identical structures have sharp tips. The dark "nectar-guides" combined with the yellow center create a bold flower to attract bees and other flying insect pollinators.

*Sisyrinchium* can be loosely translated from the Greek to mean "hog snout." The unglamorous name is attributed to the belief that wild pigs like to root up this plant. Exotic animals such as the wild hog in the Smokies cause immense damage to the native plants.

◆ **HABITAT**—Moist fields, roadsides, balds, openings, creating dense colonies under favorable conditions.

◆ **LOCATIONS**—Cades Cove Loop Road, The Boulevard Trail.

◆ **BLOOMS APRIL - JUNE**

# MOUNTAIN SPIDERWORT

Ken Voorhis

*Tradescantia
subaspera
var. montana*

Spiderwort Family
(*Commelinaceae*)

Plant: 8"-36"
(20-92 cm)
Flower: 1"-2"
(2.5-5 cm)

Low-mid elevation
Occasional

Its long parallel-veined leaves and jointed stems lend this plant the appearance of giant spider legs. Six yellow, bearded stamens ring the center of the three-petaled blue flower. The flower opens in the morning and, if pollinated, its petals rapidly wilt, often leaving a wet residue. This strange occurrence led to a second common name, widow's tears.

Scientists use this genus for many studies because of its large chromosomes. Recently, spiderworts have been studied as natural barometers for air pollution and radiation. Severe exposure to air pollutants causes a change in flower color—the degree of blue to purple color change indicates the amount of air pollution.

◆ **HABITAT**—Dry woods.
◆ **LOCATIONS**—Greenbrier Road, Noland Divide Trail.
◆ **BLOOMS JUNE - JULY**

*Houstonia serpyllifolia*

Madder Family
(*Rubiaceae*)

Plant: 3"-5"
(8-13 cm)
Flower: ⅓"
(0.8 cm)

Wide range
Common

*side view of flower*

Ed Pomikwia

This tiny flower should never be overlooked. Four blue petals surround a central yellow spot. In places, dozens of flowers combine to form a pleasing mosaic, not only for us, but for the numerous pollinators such as bees, butterflies, and hoverflies attracted to it.

What appears as a flat disc of petals is just the tip of a very interesting blossom. Below the floral plane, the petals extend to create a smooth tube. Some tubes may have a slight bulge to encapsulate the anthers of the four long stamens. Other flowers lack this bulge for they have four short stamens. This dimorphism (two forms) is common throughout the bluet genus. Dimorphism reduces self-pollination and thus helps maintain genetic variations in the populations.

◆ **HABITAT**—Moist woods, streamsides.

◆ **LOCATIONS**—Clingmans Dome Road, The Boulevard Trail.

◆ **BLOOMS MAY - AUGUST**

# WOODLAND BLUETS

*Houstonia purpurea*

Madder Family
(*Rubiaceae*)

Plant: 6″-8″
(15-20 cm)
Flower: ½″
(1.3 cm)

Low-mid elevation
Common

Jessie M. Harris

At the peak of its slender, hairy, four-angled stem sit several clusters of flowers called cymes. This flower arrangement is composed of three or more blossoms with the central flower opening first. Each flower has four lavender-blue petals that fuse into a deep tube.

Interestingly, not all flowers on a plant are the same. Some have short stamens and long pistils; the others are just the opposite. Why? To assure cross-pollination. Carried by insects, the pollen from short stamens will be deposited on short pistils and the pollen from long stamens will be deposited on long pistils.

Bluets come in two types: those with solitary flowers and those with clusters of flowers. This is the most common of the latter.

◆ **HABITAT**—Well-drained slopes, moist woods.
◆ **LOCATIONS**—Rich Mountain Road, Porters Creek Trail.
◆ **BLOOMS MAY - JULY**

## *Erigeron pulchellus*

# ROBIN'S-PLAINTAIN

Aster Family
(*Asteraceae*)

Plant: 6"-20"
(15-51 cm)
Flower head: 1"-1½"
(2.5-3.8 cm)

Low elevation
Frequent

*ray flower*

Jessie M. Harris

Robin's-plantain has daisy-like flowers with lilac to white ray flowers (outer petals). The ray flowers are numerous (50-100), very narrow, and ¼"-½" long. There can be 1-12 flower heads. Most of the leaves are at the base of the plant. The basal leaves are spoon-shaped and slightly toothed. The stem leaves are more lance-shaped. The plant is hairy throughout. Philadelphia fleabane (*E. philadelphicus*) has flower heads that are ½" -1" wide, white rays, and upper leaves that clasp the stem. Daisy-fleabane (*E. annuus and E. strigosus*) have flowers similar to Philadelphia fleabane, but their leaves are not clasping. Horse-weed (*Conyza canadensis*) has flower heads less than ⅛" across and its rays point upward.

◆ **HABITAT**—Open, moist woods, woodland edges, and thickets.
◆ **LOCATIONS**—Balsam Mountain Road, Bradley Fork Trail.
◆ **BLOOMS APRIL - JUNE**

# HEART-LEAVED ASTER

*Aster cordifolius*

Aster Family
(*Asteraceae*)

Plant: 1'-5'
(0.3-1.5 m)
Flower head: ½"-¾"
(1.3-1.9 cm)

Wide range
Common

Joseph G. Strauch, Jr.

*disk flower*

This aster has daisy-like flower heads with 8-20 blue-violet to rose (sometimes white) rays and yellow or red disk flowers. The bracts surrounding the base of each head are green and purple-tinged. The leaves are arranged alternately up the stem, and are relatively thin and scaly in texture. All of the leaves (except for the tiniest ones in the flower cluster) are stalked, toothed, and heart-shaped at the base.

Honey bees collect both nectar and pollen from plants to feed to developing larvae in the hive. Honey made from asters, including heart-leaved aster, is dark and pungent. As a foraging bee crawls on the aster, previously collected pollen brushes off the bee and fertilizes the ray and disk flowers.

◆ **HABITAT**—Woodlands, thickets, roadsides.
◆ **LOCATIONS**—Clingmans Dome Road, Schoolhouse Gap Trail.
◆ **BLOOMS SEPTEMBER - OCTOBER**

Bellflower Family
(*Campanulaceae*)

Plant: 12"-36"
(30-92 cm)
Flower: ¼"-⅓"
(0.6-0.8 cm)

Low-mid elevation
Common

Harry Ellis

This wildflower may have one or several stems bearing many delicate, nodding, bell-shaped flowers. The flowers can range in color from almost white to blue to purple. The petals curl backward. The style protrudes from the blossom. Each toothed leaf tapers at both ends. They are arranged alternately along the stem. A similar plant found in the park is tall bellflower (*Campanulastrum americanum*) with flowers one inch wide on a single leafy spike.

With its open, radially symmetrical flowers, southern harebell looks vastly different than its closest relatives, the Lobelias. Adaptation to different pollinators is probably the reason these close relatives look completely different.

◆ **HABITAT**—Rocky woods and slopes, trailsides.
◆ **LOCATIONS**—Balsam Mountain Road, Schoolhouse Gap Trail.
◆ **BLOOMS JULY - OCTOBER (or frost)**

# HOG-PEANUT

*Amphicarpaea bracteata*

Pea Family
(*Fabaceae*)

Plant: twining
stems up to 3'
(92 cm)
Flower: ½"
(1.3 cm)

Low-mid elevation
Common

Steve Kemp

Though hog-peanut is a common wildflower in the park, it is easily overlooked because of its inconspicuous flower and its habit of crawling and twining on other plants. Its flowers vary in color from pale lilac to white. The leaves are divided into three leaflets, with each leaflet being egg-shaped, pointed at the end, and untoothed.

Hog-peanut has two types of flowers. Those described above are open and promote cross-fertilization by attracting insect pollinators. But the plant also has cleistogamous flowers that never open, are self-fertilized, and are underground. The pods produced from these flowers are fleshy, underground, and one-seeded. It is from these flowers and seed pods that the plant gets its common name.

◆ **HABITAT**—Thickets and moist woods.

◆ **LOCATIONS**—Cades Cove Loop Road, Schoolhouse Gap Trail.

◆ **BLOOMS JULY - SEPTEMBER**

*Phacelia bipinnatifida*

# PURPLE PHACELIA

Waterleaf Family
(*Hydrophyllaceae*)

Plant: 1'-2'
(.3-.6 m)
Flower: 1"
(2.5 cm)

Low-mid elevation
Occasional

Kevin Adams

Purple phacelia is the tallest of the four phacelia species found in the park. The lavender-blue flowers sit atop hairy, glandular stems. The leaves are 2"-3" long and are divided into segments along a common axis. Each segment is then lobed or cleft. Purple phacelia can be easily distinguished from Pursh's purple phacelia (*P. purshii*) by the short fringes present on the latter. Look for that infrequently encountered species in moist, open meadows and roadsides.

Purple phacelia is more commonly found in the central portions of North America. Park populations are at the eastern edge of their native range. Like most other members of this genus, purple phacelia is very attractive when forming large colonies.

◆ **HABITAT**—Rocky woods.
◆ **LOCATIONS**—Laurel Creek Road, Chestnut Top Trail.
◆ **BLOOMS APRIL - MAY**

# CLINGMAN'S HEDGE-NETTLE

Harry Ellis

*Stachys
clingmanii*

Mint Family
(*Lamiaceae*)

Plant: 18″-30″
(46-76 cm)
Flower: ½″-¾″
(1.3-1.9 cm)

Mid-high elevation
Frequent

The small flowers are found in clusters at the base of the upper leaves, or in a spike at the top of the stem. The blossoms are pink or lavender and spotted with purple. The toothed leaves are heart-shaped at the base of the plant and gradually reduced upwards. The stem is angled and quite hairy. Other species found in the park are: hairy hedge-nettle (*S. nuttallii*), whose leaves are abruptly reduced upwards on the plant, and rough hedge-nettle (*S. tenuifolia* var. *latidens*) which has rounded rather than heart-shaped leaves.

Despite its common name, this is a mint, not a nettle. The specific name, "clingmanii," refers to its place of discovery, Clingmans Dome in the park. It lives only in the southern Appalachians.

◆ **HABITAT**—Moist woods, thickets, and grassy balds.
◆ **LOCATIONS**—Balsam Mountain Road, Clingmans Dome Trail.
◆ **BLOOMS JUNE - AUGUST**

*Aconitum uncinatum*

Buttercup Family
(*Ranunculaceae*)

Plant: 2'-4'
(0.6-1.2 m)
Flower: ¾"-1"
(1.9-2.5 cm)

Wide range
Occasional

Jessie M. Harris

The deep-purple flowers of this plant grow at the top of a tall slender stem. The stem seems unable to hold up under this flowering burden and is often bent over or propped against other plants. Five sepals combine to form the hood-like blossom. Two petals have nectaries tucked deep into this hood. This arrangement is designed to facilitate pollination by bumblebees. The lower sepals provide a landing pad while the others constrict the bee's path to the hidden nectar. The insect is therefore forced past stamens and pistils.

Broad, somewhat maple-like leaves are alternately arranged along the stem. Although this plant is very poisonous, the heart and nerve sedative Aconite is derived from it.

◆ **HABITAT**—Seeps and streamsides.
◆ **LOCATIONS**—Balsam Mountain Road, The Boulevard Trail.
◆ **BLOOMS JULY - SEPTEMBER**

# MONKEY FLOWER

*Mimulus ringens L.*

Snapdragon Family
(*Scrophulariaceae*)

Plant: 1'-3'
(0.3-1.3 m)
Flower: ¾"-2"
(19-45 mm)

Low-mid elevation
Scarce

Jessie M. Harris

Look for monkey flower growing in wet meadows and along streambanks. It is a tall wildflower (up to 3') with opposite, stalk-less, serrate leaves on a squarish stem. The leaves are progressively smaller from the base to the top of the plant, and those at the top often clasp the stem. Solitary lavender to blue (rarely white) flowers are borne on 1" pedicels that curve upward. The flowers are strongly 2-lipped, and the throat of the flower tube is shaded with yellow and nearly closed. Bumblebees (*Bombus* spp.) are the primary pollinator of monkey flowers, and bees visiting the flower can forage for sugary nectar, protein-rich pollen, or both.

◆ **HABITAT**—Wet places (marshes, bogs, wet meadows, bottomlands).

◆ **LOCATION**—Abrams Creek in Cades Cove.

◆ **BLOOMS JUNE - SEPTEMBER**

## *Ruellia caroliniensis*

# CAROLINA RUELLIA

Acanthus Family
(*Acanthaceae*)

Plant: extremely
variable, to 3′
(1m)
Flower: 1″-2″
(2.5-5 cm)

Low elevations
Infrequent

*seed dispersion*

Jessie M. Harris

An alternate common name for this plant is Carolina wild petunia, and its spectacular flower does resemble the unrelated garden plant. Its funnel-shaped lavender-blue blossoms have 5 flaring lobes. Note the spiny, linear lobes of the calyx at the base of the flower. The leaves are elliptic to oval, short stalked, and arranged in pairs along the stem. The overall size of the plant is variable—along mown roadsides it will bloom when only 2″-3″ high; in forests it typically blooms when 1′-3′ tall. The plant has an interesting adaptation for dispersing its seeds. As the seed capsule dehydrates, tiny hook-like projections (jaculators) on the interior wall of the capsule twist and eject the seeds from the parent plant. Most other plants of the genus *Ruellia* are tropical.

◆ **HABITAT**— Dry to moist forests, clearings, roadsides.

◆ **LOCATION**—Hazel Creek Trail.

◆ **BLOOMS MAY - SEPTEMBER**

# ADAM-AND-EVE ORCHID

Jessie M. Harris

*Aplectrum hyemale*

Orchid Family
(*Orchidaceae*)

Plant: 1'-2'
(.3-.6 m)
Flower: 1"
(2.5 cm)

Low-mid elevation
Frequent

*winter leaf*

This orchid can be enjoyed in two seasons. In autumn, the attractive, solitary leaf emerges. The following spring the plant blossoms. The leaf is distinctive: narrowly oval, 4"-7" long and 1"-3" wide, pleated, dark green with conspicuous white veins. The leaf fades in early spring, before the leafless flowering stalk appears. There can be 6-20 flowers on the stalk. The flowers can be difficult to see against the forest floor because they are greenish-purplish.

The common name for the plant comes from the structure of the root: roundish balls ("corms") connected by fibers. Each corm lasts about two years, so they are found in pairs—Adam and Eve. "*Hyemale*" means "of winter," alluding to the winter-green leaf.

◆ **HABITAT**—Moist woods.
◆ **LOCATIONS**—Newfound Gap Road, Lower Mt. Cammerer Trail.
◆ **BLOOMS MAY - JUNE**

*Tipularia discolor*

# CRANE-FLY ORCHID

Orchid Family
(*Orchidaceae*)

Plant: 8"-16"
(20-40 cm)
Flower: ½"
(1.3 cm)

Low-mid elevation
Frequent

*winter leaf*

Harry Ellis

This orchid is most easily identified by its distinctive leaf (although it is not present when the plant blooms). This orchid's species name, *discolor*, refers to the two-colored leaf: green on top and purple below. The solitary leaf also makes this a "backwards" plant as it emerges in late summer and vanishes the next spring. The flowering stalk, produced at midsummer with no leaves at all, bears up to two dozen blossoms. The bronze flowers can be difficult to spot against the leaf litter of the forest.

There are only two species of crane-fly orchid in the world, ours and another found in the Himalayas. Crane-fly orchid is one of the most common orchids in the park, and it is often seen along trails.

◆ **HABITAT**—Moist woods.
◆ **LOCATIONS**—Cades Cove Loop Road, Lower Mt. Cammerer Tr.
◆ **BLOOMS JULY - SEPTEMBER**

# HEAL-ALL

*Prunella vulgaris*

Mint Family
*(Lamiaceae)*

Plant: less than 12″
(30 cm)
Flower: many small
flowers in cylindrical
spikes 1″-2″ long, 1″
in diameter

Wide range
Frequent

Joseph G. Strauch, Jr.

This is a woodland plant that is also common along trails and road-sides. Heal-all is variable in habit (creeping or erect), foliage, and size of floral spike. Commonly, it is a low-growing, sprawling plant. The blue-violet flowers are in cylindrical spikes 1″-2″ long and 1″ in diameter. The green, leafy tube surrounding each individual flower is hairy. Heal-all leaves are paired along the stem. Leaves may be toothed or untoothed, egg-shaped or lance-shaped.

As its common name implies, heal-all was used medicinally. It was thought to be particularly effective for diseases of the mouth, probably because the small opening between the upper and lower petals resembles a mouth.

♦ **HABITAT**—Woodland edges, trailsides, streamsides.
♦ **LOCATIONS**—Newfound Gap Road, Bradley Fork Trail.
♦ **BLOOMS APRIL - OCTOBER**

*Conoclinium
coelestinum*

Aster Family
(*Asteraceae*)

Plant: 1'-3'
(0.3-1 m)
Flower: ⅕" to ⅓"
(5-8 mm)

Low-mid elevation
Occasional

Jessie M. Harris

Don't mistake this native wildflower for garden ageratum. Like its domestic relatives, mistflower is in the Aster family. Mistflower favors moist, disturbed areas and streambanks. It is colonial, using slender rhizomes (underground branches) to spread. In autumn, mistflower's tiny seeds (each with fluffy pappus) disperse in the wind. The plant can vary greatly in height, but is usually about knee-high. Scalloped leaves with prominent lateral veins are arranged oppositely on the stiff stem. Each flower head is composed of 35-70 minute tubular flowers, so a plant with dozens of flower heads will have literally thousands of flowers! Though not especially common in the park, it is conspicuous because there are few other blue or purple wildflowers that bloom when it does.

◆ **HABITAT**—Streambanks and moist, disturbed habitats.
◆ **BLOOMS JULY - OCTOBER**

# STIFF GENTIAN

*Gentianella quinquefolia*

Gentian Family
*(Gentianaceae)*

Plant: 6"-30"
(1½-8 dm)
Flower: ½"-1"
(1½-2½ cm)

Wide range
Occasional

Jessie M. Harris

Stiff gentian is spectacular in bloom, and since it favors roadbanks, woodland borders, and stream margins, hikers are unlikely to miss it if they happen upon a population. Stiff gentian is an annual that can vary in height (6"-30") and in the amount of branching (2 or 3 to dozens). The leaves are paired, stalkless, and have prominent veins on the undersides. Dense clusters of flowers terminate the branches. The petals are united into a tube at the base, and terminate in 5 short lobes. The color of the petals can vary from deep violet to lilac to white. Like its alpine cousins, stiff gentian is adapted to cold, and the flowers tolerate chilly autumn nights well. The bitter-tasting root is used by some to treat poor appetite, intestinal worms, and fevers.

- ◆ **HABITAT**—Roadbanks, woodland borders, streambanks.
- ◆ **LOCATION**—Polls Gap.
- ◆ **BLOOMS LATE AUGUST - OCTOBER**

# PASSION-FLOWER, MAY-POP

## *Passiflora incarnata*

Passionflower Family
(*Passifloraceae*)

Plant: vines up to
several yards (meters)
Flower: 3"
(8 cm)

Low elevation
Scarce

Jessie M. Harris

Follow the sprawling vine to find the remarkably complex flowers and aromatic fruit. The flowers harbor a secret—they have evolved for their insect partners. The hallmark of the Passion-flower family is the floral corona—filaments that extend outward like a cup—which is not only a visual attractor for insect pollinators, but also a landing platform, perfumery, and nectary. The plant even attracts and feeds defenders: a pair of glands on each leaf stalk (just below the base of the 3-lobed leaf) exude a sweet liquid rich in amino acids that attracts ants and wasps to protect the plant from herbivores. The 2"-3" long yellow-green fruit, commonly called a "may-pop," holds seeds. Each seed has a fleshy, intensely aromatic, edible appendage (aril).

◆ **HABITAT**—Meadows, trailsides, thickets.
◆ **LOCATION**—Metcalf Bottoms.
◆ **BLOOMS MAY - JULY**

# SWEET JOE-PYE-WEED  *Eupatorium purpureum*

Aster Family
(*Asteraceae*)

Plant: 3'-10'
(0.9-3 m)
Flower head:
⅛"wide (.3 cm)

Low-mid elevation
Common

Ed Ponikwia

Use all your senses to appreciate this robust wildflower. The plant is tall and the leaves are in whorls of 3-4. The stem is greenish, then dark purple at the nodes where the leaf whorls are. Gently scrape the stem with your fingernail and smell the vanilla odor. Rub a leaf and note that it is toothed and slightly hairy. The cluster of flower heads is rounded, highly branched, and 3"-12" across.

Sweet Joe-Pye-weed is a popular garden plant, not only because of its wonderful size and showy flower cluster, but also because it attracts beautiful pollinators. Tiger swallowtail, monarch, red admiral, and painted lady butterflies will nectar simultaneously on a single flower cluster.

◆ **HABITAT**—Open woods and slopes.
◆ **LOCATIONS**—Cades Cove Loop Road, Little River Trail.
◆ BLOOMS JULY - SEPTEMBER

## *Caulophyllum thalictroides*

Barberry Family
(*Berberidaceae*)

Plant: 1'-3'
(.3-1 m)
Flower: ½"
(1.3 cm)

Low-mid elevation
Frequent

*seeds*

Harry Ellis

The "blue" of the common name is due to the bluish tinge of the leaves and the color of the seeds, not the flowers. The inflorescence is a stalked, loosely clustered collection of several small purplish-brown to yellow-green flowers. Each flower has six pointed sepals compli-mented by six hooded petals. The petals harbor nectar glands that attract pollinating insects. The seeds could be confused with a berry because of their deep blue coloration in late summer.

The Cherokee used blue cohosh to treat fevers, rheumatism, fits, hysteria, colic and nerves. Applying a steep of the leaves to the skin was said to alleviate the effects of poison ivy. The only other species in the genus *Caulophyllum* is native to Asia.

◆ **HABITAT**—Rich, moist woods.
◆ **LOCATIONS**—Balsam Mtn. Road, Lower Mt. Cammerer Trail.
◆ **BLOOMS APRIL-MAY**

# WILD GINGER

*Asarum canadense*

Birthwort Family
(*Aristolochiaceae*)

Plant: 6″-10″
(15-25 cm)
Flower:1½″wide
(3.8 cm)

Low-mid elevation
Common

Ken Voorhis

Twin, heart-shaped leaves rising up to 10″ off the forest floor identify this plant. These thick leaves hide the blossom beneath. A drab, but interesting, three-lobed brown flower is attached at the junction of the leaf petioles. It may be further hidden by leaf litter.

Under the leaves is where pollination is most likely to happen. Wild ginger's odor attracts female fungus gnats into the blossom where they lay their eggs. Pollen is exchanged as the gnats go from plant to plant. The ginger's poisonous tissue kills the gnat larvae as they feed, thus allowing the plant's seeds to develop safely.

Native Americans and European settlers used this plant to treat sore throats and for the ginger-like flavor of its roots.

◆ **HABITAT**—Rich, usually rocky, moist woods.
◆ **LOCATIONS**—Newfound Gap Road, Cooper Road Trail.
◆ **BLOOMS APRIL - MAY**

# *Epifagus virginiana*

Broom-rape Family
(*Orobanchaceae*)

Plant: 3"-15"
(8-40 cm)
Flower: ¼"
 (1 cm)

Wide range
Frequent

Jessie M. Harris

If you are near an American beech tree and find reddish-brown twigs seemingly sprouting from the forest floor, stop and take a closer look! You may have found beechdrops, a native wildflower. Beechdrops, like all other members of the Broom-rape family, lacks chlorophyll (green pigment) and is wholly parasitic, stealing nutrients from the roots of beech trees. The plant's scientific name reflects this: *epi* (upon) and *fagus* (beech tree.) It has leaves that are reduced to mere scales, and numerous ¼"-long flowers. The whole plant is pale reddish-brown in color during the growing season, then dries to dark brown in winter. There is only one species of beechdrops, and it is found throughout eastern North America.

◆ **HABITAT**—Rich woods under beech trees.
◆ **LOCATION**—Ramsey Cascades Trail.
◆ **BLOOMS SEPTEMBER - NOVEMBER**

# LITTLE BROWN JUGS

*Hexastylis arifolia*

Birthwort Family
(*Aristolochiaceae*)

Plant: 4"-6"
(10-15 cm)
Flower: ½"
(1.3 cm)

Low-mid elevation
Frequent

Jessie M. Harris

Little brown jugs can be found by searching for their distinctive leaves which are leathery, evergreen, and arrowhead-shaped. The "arrow barbs" account for ⅓ of the leaf's 3"-4" length. Beneath the leaves are the small, three-lobed, jug-shaped blossoms. Like the related wild ginger, this plant is sometimes pollinated by fungus gnats.

Spotted little brown jugs (*H. shuttleworthii*) can be found in the lower Abrams Creek area. It has smaller, more heart-shaped leaves. White markings follow the veins of spotted little brown jug leaves; on *H. arifolia*, the markings are between the veins.

A tea brewed from this stem was also used to treat whooping cough. Modern science finds some effective antibiotics in the plant.

◆ **HABITAT**—Woodlands.

◆ **LOCATIONS**—Rich Mountain Road, Cooper Road Trail.

◆ **BLOOMS MARCH - MAY**

*Prenanthes
altissima*

Aster Family
(*Asteraceae*)

Plant: 2'-4'
(0.6-1.2 m)
Flower head: ¼"
(.6 cm)

Wide range
Common

Jessie M. Harris

The largest leaves are on the lower part of the stem, and they are exceedingly variable in shape. The branched cluster of flower heads is at the top of the plant and the heads point downwards. The bracts at the base of the flower head are greenish to purplish. There are usually less than eight straw-colored ray flowers per head.

Another Rattlesnakeroot (*P. serpentaria*) has black dots on the bracts. Lion's foot (*P. trifoliata*) has 9-13 flowers per head. Roan's rattlesnakeroot (*P. roanensis*) has stiff, dark hairs on the stem and bracts and is found only at the high elevatons.

Like many members of the Aster family, this species' seeds are wind dispersed. They float through the air on parachute-like hairs.

◆ **HABITAT**—Woodlands.

◆ **LOCATIONS**—Clingmans Dome Road, Gregory Ridge Trail.

◆ **BLOOMS AUGUST - FROST**

# INDIAN CUCUMBER
*Medeola virginiana*

Lily family
*(Liliaceae)*

Plant: 12"-36"
(30-92 cm)
Flower: ¾"
(1.9 cm)

Wide range
Common

Ed Pomikwia

A distinctive arrangement of leaves makes this late spring blooming perennial easy to identify even when not in bloom. Five to 20 leaves grow in a whorl about halfway up the single stem, with a smaller whorl of three leaves at the top of the stem (sterile stems have just one whorl). Several rather inconspicuous spidery flowers with a greenish-yellow cast nod below the uppermost set of leaves. Each has 3-8 petals that curl back to reveal three long brown stamens curving outwards. Autumn berry colors include red, black, blue and purple. The berries stand upright on a short stalk over the leaves.

This plant's white, underground rhizomes were a favored food of Native Americans and early settlers.

◆ **HABITAT**—Moist woods.
◆ **LOCATIONS**—Rich Mountain Road, Lower Mt. Cammerer Trail.
◆ **BLOOMS APRIL - JUNE**

# FALSE HELLEBORE

Bunchflower Family
*(Melanthiaceae)*

Plant: 2'-8'
(0.6-2.4 m)
Flower: ½"-¾"
(1.3-1.9 cm)

High elevation
Frequent

Harry Ellis

The large, heavily ribbed leaves are the most distinctive feature of this highly poisonous plant. A dense cluster of many yellow-green flowers are borne on an erect, but branching stalk. Star-shaped and hairy, each individual flower has three sepals and three petals. The fruit, which appears quickly after the petals have faded, is an egg shaped capsule containing numerous winged seeds.

Beware of this plant—each year people mistake it for an edible and either die or must undergo a liver transplant. Although not without dangerous side effects, it has proven useful in controlling hypertension by depressing the heart rate. Several pharmaceutical preparations still incorporate the false hellebore.

◆ **HABITAT**—Seepage areas, moist thickets.
◆ **LOCATIONS**—Heintooga Ridge Road, Gregory Bald Trail.
◆ **BLOOMS MAY - JULY**

# ALUMROOT

*Heuchera americana*

Saxifrage Family
(*Saxifragaceae*)

Plant: flowering
stalk 1'-2'
(.3-.6 m)
Flower: ¼" pro-
truding stamens
(0.6 cm)

Low-mid elevation
Frequent

Rob and Ann Simpson

The flowering stalk of alumroot is knee-high and usually leafless. Stamens protrude from each small greenish-purple flower. Each leaf has a long stalk and grows from the base of the plant. The leaves are shallowly lobed, toothed, and heart-shaped at the base. *H. villosa* (frequent) is also found in the park in similar habitats. It blooms from summer to fall and has long hairs on its stems. The leaves of alumroot resemble foamflower (*Tiarella cordifolia*).

Alumroot gets its common name from the astringent qualities of the root. It is a member of the Saxifrage family, which in turn, gets its name from two Latin words meaning "rock" and "break." Many plants in the Saxifrage family grow on rocky mountainsides and cliffs.

♦ **HABITAT**—Dry, upland woods and rocky hillsides.
♦ **LOCATIONS**—Rich Mountain Road, Chestnut Top Trail.
♦ **BLOOMS APRIL - JUNE**

# JACK-IN-THE-PULPIT

Arum Family
(*Araceae*)

Plant: 12"-36"
(30-92 cm)
Pulpit: 2"-6"
(5-15 cm)

Wide range
Common

*flowers at base
of "Jack"*

Jessie M. Harris

If you get on your knees and look closely at this unusual plant you should be able to recognize the hooded pulpit and "Jack," the minister, standing within it. The true flowers are tiny and clustered around the feet of "Jack." The "pulpit," called a spathe, may be green or brownish-purple, and can be striped or mottled. By late summer, a cluster of bright crimson berries appear and almost all traces of the pulpit are gone. Some Jack-in-the-pulpits are all male, others all female, and still others have both sexes. There are either one or two leaves, each divided into three leaflets.

This plant's maroon color and carrion odor are clues that it is pollinated by flies.

◆ **HABITAT**—Moist woods.
◆ **LOCATIONS**—Tremont Road, Porters Creek Trail.
◆ **BLOOMS MARCH - JUNE**

# WHORLED POGONIA

*Isotria verticillata*

Orchid Family
(*Orchidaceae*)

Plant: 4″-12″
(9-35 cm)
Flower: 4,″ including
spreading sepals
(10 cm)

Low-mid elevation
Scarce

Jessie M. Harris

Whorled pogonia is one of the better camouflaged orchids: sterile plants strongly resemble Indian cucumber, and flowering plants blend in well with the sun-dappled forest floor. This orchid propagates from short rhizomes, so you will likely find several plants in close proximity. The single stem is smooth, succulent, and usually reddish brown or purple in color. The stem bears a single whorl of 5 leaves (infrequently 6-10 leaves) near the summit and 1 (sometimes 2) terminal flowers. The leaves point upward while the flower is blooming. The three widely spreading sepals are purplish-brown and tapered toward the tips. The 2 yellow-green lateral petals point forward, and together with the lip, form a tube. The central lobe of the lip has purple veining.

♦ **HABITAT**—Dry, acidic soil in oak-pine woods.
♦ **LOCATION**—Smokemont Loop Trail.
♦ **BLOOMS APRIL-JULY**

*Arisaema dracontium*

Arum Family
(*Araceae*)

Plant: 18″-36″
(0.5-1 m)
Flower: spadix 3″-5″
(8-12 cm)
spathe 1″-2″
(3-5 cm)

Low elevation
Rare

Rob and Ann Simpson

Think of green dragon as a Jack-in-the-pulpit with an attitude. Instead of a demure Jack hiding in his leafy pulpit, green dragon has a claw that protrudes out of a leafy sheath! The claw is the upper, naked, sterile portion of the fleshy spadix; the fertile, flower-bearing portion of the spadix is at the base. The leafy sheath, the spathe, is usually an inch or two (3-5 cm) long and protects the flowers. The berries ripen red in mid-summer. Green dragon has a solitary leaf with 7-15 pointy leaf segments arranged in a crescent. The flowers are pollinated by insects—particularly flies and beetles—that are attracted by the flowers' disagreeable odor. Don't sample the fruit or foliage—it will bite back! All parts of green dragon contain toxic calcium oxalate crystals.

◆ **HABITAT**—Moist woods.
◆ **LOCATION**—Abrams Creek in Cades Cove.
◆ **BLOOMS MAY**

# ILLUSTRATED GLOSSARY

## Leaves

*alternate arrangement*

*opposite arrangement*

*compound leaf (6 leaflets)*

*whorled arrangement*

*cordate shape*

## Flowers

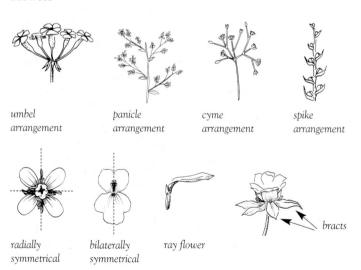

*umbel arrangement*

*panicle arrangement*

*cyme arrangement*

*spike arrangement*

*radially symmetrical*

*bilaterally symmetrical*

*ray flower*

*bracts*

# GLOSSARY

ALTERNATE. Growing singly along the stem; usually applied to describe the arrangement of leaves on stem

ANNUAL. A plant that goes through its life cycle in one growing season. The plant starts as a seedling, then matures, produces flowers and seeds, and dies

ANTHER. Terminal, pollen-producing portion of stamen

AXIL. The point where two structures meet; usually applied to the point where a leaf joins a stem

BASAL. At the base, or bottom, of the plant

BIENNIAL. A plant that completes its life cycle in two growing seasons or two years

BILATERAL SYMMETRY. Applied to irregular flowers in which the petals are dissimilar in size, shape and spacing so that there is a single plane of symmetry producing left and right mirror images

BRACT. A leaf just underneath a flower, flower cluster, or branch; a bract is usually smaller and is different in shape, color or texture from the plant's other leaves

CALYX. Collective name for a set of sepals of a flower; the sepals are sometimes fused to form a calyx tube

CAPSULE. A dry seed-containing structure; dry fruit developed from two or more carpels (pistils)

CARPEL. A single pistil or one member of a compound pistil; ovules (immature egg cells) are found in the carpels

CHLOROPHYLL. Green pigment found in plants that enables it to use solar energy to make sugars

CLEISTOGAMOUS FLOWER. Closed flower; a specialized type of self-pollinating flower that never opens and is usually inconspicuous

COMPOUND. Composed of multiple similar parts; usually applied to leaves that are divided into separate leaflets

CORDATE. Heart-shaped

COROLLA. Collective name for the whorl of petals in a flower

CYME. A broad, branched inflorescence in which pedicels are all the same length

DISK FLOWER. An urn-shaped flower found in the Aster family; the flowers in the center or "eye" of a sunflower are disk flowers

DISSECTED. Divided into many segments

ELLIPTIC. A shape (usually applied to leaves) that is an elongated circle, narrowed at both ends, and widest at the middle

ENDEMIC. A species that is restricted to a particular geographic region

ENTIRE. Having an edge without lobes or teeth; usually used to describe a leaf margin

EPHEMERAL. Appearing for only a short time; spring ephemerals grow and bloom for a few weeks then die completely (for annuals) or die back to the ground level (for perennials) until the next spring

FLOWER. A structure that contains either carpels (pistils) or stamens or both, usually surrounded by calyx (sepals) or corolla (petals) or both

GENUS. The taxonomic rank below family and above species; the generic name is always capitalized and underlined or italicized; "genera" the plural

GLOBULAR. Round; globe-like

INFLORESCENCE. The cluster of flowers on a plant

LANCE-SHAPED A shape that is longer than wide, with the widest portion at the base and tapering gradually to the tip; usually applied to the shape of a leaf or petal

LEAF MARGIN. The edge of the leaf

LEAFLET. Single blade of a compound leaf

LINEAR. Long and narrow, with the sides nearly parallel; usually used to describe leaf and petal shape

NECTAR. Sweet fluid produced by flowers used to attract animal pollinators; honey bees collect, digest, and concentrate nectar to make honey

NECTARY. Nectar-secreting gland

NODE. Point at which leaves or flowers occur along a stem

OPPOSITE. Growing in pairs along the stem; usually applied to the arrangement of leaves

OVARY. Part of a pistil that contains the ovules (immature, unfertilized egg cells)

PANICLE. An elongated inflorescence with stalked flowers

PEDICEL. Flower stalk

PERENNIAL. A plant that lives for more than two growing seasons; herbaceous perennials die back seasonally to rhizomes, tubers, corms, or bulbs

PETALS. Specialized structures surrounding and protecting the reproductive organs of a plant; some flowers lack petals, some have inconspicuous petals, some have brightly colored petals to attract animal pollinators

PETIOLE. Leaf stalk (stem); a sessile leaf lacks a petiole

PISTIL. Female, seed-producing organ of the flower; a pistil is composed of the "ovary" (contains immature seeds), the "style" (stalk above the ovary), and the "stigma" (the tip)

POLLEN. Dust-like particles that contain the plant's male sex cells

POLLINATORS. Animals (usually insects and birds) that spread pollen from plant to plant

RADIAL SYMMETRY. Petals or petal-like parts are arranged around a center like the spokes on a wheel; each petal (or petal-like part) is similar in size, shape and spacing to the others so there are multiple axes of symmetry

RAY FLOWER. A petal-like flower found in the Aster family; the flowers around the perimeter of a sunflower are ray flowers

RECEPTACLE. The enlarged flower stalk (pedicel) where the bracts and/or flower parts are attached

RECURVED. Bent or curved, usually backward or downward

RHIZOME. Underground (or sub-surface) stem that grows horizontally; the leaves of a rhizome are usually reduced to scales

ROSETTE. A tight cluster of leaves radiating from a central point; rosettes are usually found at the base of a plant

SEPALS. Specialized leaves surrounding and protecting the reproductive organs of a plant; a flower may lack sepals, have green sepals, or have brightly colored sepals

SERRATE. Saw-toothed; usually used to describe a leaf margin

SESSILE. Without a stalk, petiole, or pedicel; sitting directly on a stem

SPECIES. The taxonomic rank below genus; specific names are not capitalized

SPIKE. An elongated inflorescence with stalkless flowers

STALK. The "stem" of a leaf (more accurately termed "petiole"), or flower (more accurately termed "pedicel")

STAMEN. Male organ of the flower; a stamen is composed of the "filament," or stalk, and "anther," the sac at the filament's tip which produces pollen

STEM. A structure that bears leaves, though those leaves may be reduced to scales; stems may be above-ground or below-ground (see rhizome and tuber)

STIGMA. The sticky tip of the pistil that catches pollen

STIPULES. Small leaf-like structures at the base of a leaf; leafy stipules are common in the Rose family

STYLE. Part of the pistil; usually a stalk-like structure connecting the ovary and stigma

TENDRIL. Slender twining structure (modified from a leaf or stem) that enables plants to climb; tendrils are common in the Pea family (*Fabaceae*)

TERMINAL. Last; most distal; top-most

TUBER. A thick, short stem that is usually underground; the common potato is an example of a tuber

UMBEL. An inflorescence in which the flower stalks (pedicels) originate from the same point so that the flower cluster resembles an umbrella

WHORL. A circle; three or more leaves or flowers encircling a stem

WILDFLOWER. A naturally-growing flowering plant that is not woody

# SPECIES INDEX

# OTHER GUIDES TO THE SMOKIES

## BIRDS OF THE SMOKIES
by Fred J. Alsop, III
This extraordinary guide includes 100 color photos of park birds and a detailed text which reflects over 25 years of birding in the Smokies. It tells where to find birds, includes suggested birding trips, a bird song guide, a complete checklist, and a special "how to" section on the park's 12 most sought after species. 167 pages, 4.5" x 6" **$10.95**.

## TREES OF THE SMOKIES
by Steve Kemp
A delightful, pocket-sized field guide to the trees of the area. Features 80 color photographs of the most common species along with over 100 line drawings. Text covers virgin forests, record trees, blooming times, fall colors, plus a complete key and checklist. 128 pages, 4.5" x 6" **$8.95**.

## HIKING TRAILS OF THE SMOKIES
The first comprehensive guide to the official trails of Great Smoky Mountains National Park. Covers all 149 trails with in-depth narratives and special trail profile charts (show how steep each mile is). Includes sections on suggested loop hikes, medical emergencies, backcountry registration. Full color trail map included! 580 pages, 4.5" x 6", 11 ounces **$17.95**.

Books are available at all park visitor centers or by contacting Great Smoky Mountains Association, 115 Park Headquarters Road, Gatlinburg, TN (865) 436-0120, www.SmokiesStore.org. Proceeds from sales support park programs and services.

"To see a World in a Grain of Sand
And a Heaven in a Wild Flower..."

-William Blake

"Earth Laughs in Flowers"

-Ralph Waldo Emerson